W9-CSC-981

CONDUCT EXPECTED

CONDUCT EXPECTED

*The Unwritten Rules
for a Successful
Business Career*

by

William Lareau

NEW CENTURY PUBLISHERS, INC.

Printing Code
11   12   13   14   15   16   17

Library of Congress Cataloging in Publication Data

Lareau, William.
   Conduct expected.

   1. Success in business.   2. Business etiquette.
I. Title.
HF5386.L26   1985   650.1   84-27280
ISBN 0-8329-0388-4

DEDICATION

To my wife, Darlene, who coaxed this book out of me by masterfully applying the principles of Chapter 7 while always permitting me to believe that she was employing the techniques discussed in Chapter 6.

Contents

Dedication

Introduction

INTRODUCTION

Hundreds of books purport to tell you how to increase your chances of success in the business world. Many of these books contain valuable nuggets of information. The problem is that you're seldom told specifically what to do in a given situation. Most of the time you're treated to a general discussion of the issues and then told to make a 'wise choice'. Thanks for the help! You probably already know many of the underlying principles of human behavior and organization dynamics. Trying to figure them out and apply them in the midst of the chaos of a typical business day is another story. What's needed is a set of heuristics that can be applied without a lot of situational analysis every time something happens or is about to happen. This book was written to supply such straightforward guidelines.

There's another serious deficit in the typical business success book. If you've been out there working, you know or suspect that the business world is one sorry state of messed-up affairs. It's no different from any other aspect of human and animal life: surprises, disasters, and stupidity are the rule rather than the exception. You'd never know it by reading the standard newspapers, journals, and self-congratulatory hype produced by academics, executives, and consultants. It's about time for someone to call a disorganized mess a disorganized mess and to tell you how to survive in the midst of it.

CONDUCT EXPECTED will show you how to optimize your chances in the business world as it really is, not as every organization's glossy annual report would have you believe it is.

This book doesn't tell you how to achieve self-actualization and fulfillment at work (don't try: it's impossible) or in your personal life (try very hard, but you'll have to look elsewhere for detailed instructions). This book is written for those who are out to make your mark in business and who will do anything reasonable to get there. I've structured the presentation from the more general and fundamental to the specific. For example, the first chapter gives what I regard as a realistic and practical perspective on business and life in general. What I call Hard Facts provide the foundation for what follows: the rules, detailed instructions regarding all aspects of business behavior and demeanor.

The orientation of this book's presentation is intended to be interesting and rewarding. I've been working as a psychologist, consultant, and operational manager in various areas of the business world for almost twenty years, and I thought I knew a lot about how to act and what to do (not that I always followed my own advice). The experience of having to distill practical, no-nonsense heuristics from the mass of existing theory, applied knowledge, and the way things in business actually operate (or, more often, don't operate) forced me to view business behaviors in many new and sometimes disturbing ways. Very often theorists and management-development specialists ignore reality when they're writing books and/or installing systems in an organization. At the same time, most managers and executives totally ignore the very real effects of individuals' social needs and the very strong influences of group and organization dynamics as they try to influence and direct large groups of employees. Some solid research has been done in social psychology. The Appendices give my treatment of the relevant information from the literature of group dynamics, organization theory, and behavior and modification principles. I urge you to go beyond the Rules and examine this material. I've presented it as an aid to your deeper understanding so that you can more effectively follow the Rules. This book's presentation throws out the theoretical nonsense and gets to the heart of the matter: how organizations and the people in them behave, and how you can best take advantage of their behaviors and expectations in order to attain your career goals.

I hope that your exposure to this book's viewpoint and these specific Rules helps you to reach the goals you have set for yourself. Knowing the Rules isn't enough, however, so I've included a chapter that provides a relatively simple way of implementing your own behavior modification program. The critical element is recording and scoring each days' behavior on forms provided, each dealing with a specific performance area. A regularly scheduled review of what you do on the job, as well as what you think and feel, will heighten your awareness and permit you to more effectively follow the rules and increase your chances of success.

CONDUCT EXPECTED

1

Straight Talk Right from the Start

You picked up this book because you want to make it big in the business world. You hope that maybe—just maybe—this time you'll find the answer. You think that if you could get a little advantage, just show a little more business savvy than the next person, you'd finally be recognized as the raging business dynamo you know you could be if you just had half a chance. You've read all the latest and fashionable books on how the business world operates, how to pick a wardrobe that will lead to success, how companies pursue excellence, and how to do anything to or with an employee in a limited period of time. Yet you still haven't found the answer. You continue to buy "business success" books because you keep hoping you'll stumble across a technique or approach that fits with the way you already do your work. You're looking for something that will let you continue to do just about what you've always done but with a few minor and easy changes that will enable you to become a business success.

Well, the plain, immutable truth is that there is no easy way to be a success in the business world without a lot of boring, mundane, difficult, and often disgusting and humiliating work. That's the way the business world is, and that's the way the work is.

Even though you might be willing to agree that hard work is the only way most people are going to make it big, you probably fantasize about becoming a success by means of an incredible stroke of fate. We've all heard and read the instant success stories. You're still hoping that you'll be lucky and get discovered.

The typical instant success fantasy usually involves a hero who saves

3

the company from ruin by pulling off a single act of daring personal courage or intellectual artistry. Popular variations include fantasies such as the timeless "Late-Night Discovery" (in which the lonely and frustrated top executive wanders into your office, asks your advice, takes it, saves the company, and turns the reins over to you), the "Temper Tantrum" (in which you get fed up with all the baloney at a high-level staff meeting, get up and "tell it like it is," and get put in charge by the president, who was waiting for such a display of courage and intelligence), and, finally, the always satisfying "Frank Talk" (in which you run up to the executive suite and get your boss and all your enemies fired by telling the president what a bunch of idiots they are).

Your fantasies probably follow the same general pattern. You finally get to be a big success by a bold maneuver that merely shows you as you've always been to someone with sufficient intelligence and business insight to recognize your obvious potential. People support and perpetuate such fantasies because they are afraid to admit that success requires a lot of hard and unpleasant work. A lot of people know that they don't have the discipline and energy to apply themselves long and hard enough to make it as a success. Rather than face this unpleasant and disturbing fact about themselves, they wallow in their fantasies and perpetuate stories that prove that luck is the primary element in being successful. Well, it's time to face reality. The odds of such a fantasy working out are probably more than 100,000 to one. It's not going to happen to you. If you're going to get anywhere, you'll have to stop fantasizing about divine intervention and get down to the dirty and hard work that will get you to the top.

"OK, OK," you're probably saying. "Give me a break. So I have to work hard to make it. I'll forget gimmicks, and I'll stop fantasizing. I'm willing, and I'm smart, clever, well educated, and ambitious. Why, in contrast to a lot of my colleagues and superiors, I even know how to do my job fairly well. That should be enough, right?" Don't count on it. While there are an awful lot of real fools holding down good jobs without any apparent trouble, there are also a lot of ambitious, sharp people out there who want to get to the same place you do. There isn't room at or near the top (or even halfway up) for everybody who is smart enough to want it and ambitious enough to work for it. Just wanting to be a success and having the basic tools is not enough.

So what's the answer? Why do some make it and others who are just as ambitious and intelligent don't? The difference lies in the way in which the winners present themselves to the work world. Their employees perceive them as better supervisors, their bosses perceive them as better workers, and they have a much smoother journey along the road to success. What these people have developed on their own (or were lucky enough to have learned inadvertently through childhood, school, and early business experiences) is a set of work behaviors that enables them to consistently project the most positive image of themselves to everyone around them at work. Everything these people do functions to create the best possible impression of themselves in the eyes of others. They do this by minimizing as much as possible the disturbances they create for their bosses, their employees, their peers, and the organization. For a very few lucky people, the required knowledge and skill come as natural or easily learned gifts. For the majority, they must be developed through hard work and constant vigilance. That's what the rules in this book are for: to show you how to do it.

The rules will outline the appropriate behaviors and strategies for developing the most effective perception of yourself in the eyes of all those you work with. Other people make their judgments on the basis of what they see and hear from you and about you. The largest part of their assessment of you is based not upon their evaluations of the technical merits of your work but upon their expectations of the ways you should behave and how well your behaviors appeal to their emotional needs. The rules will also show you the safest and best ways to create and maintain the outstanding perception of yourself in the eyes of others, which is absolutely essential to your business success.

This is not a book on theory. The rules present specific and detailed instructions regarding all aspects of business behavior and demeanor. For example, you probably think that it's a good idea to spend as much time around the boss as you can in order to get noticed. You may not like it, but you think it helps your career if you're constantly making creative suggestions, volunteering to help out on high-visibility projects, and remaining nearby in case you're needed. We've all seen the traffic jams of misguided middle managers which pile up around some executives' offices as they jostle and maneuver for crumbs of attention. Rule 46, "Always minimize your contact with your boss," explains why such a strategy is a big mistake. You'll be surprised and shocked to find that many of the other "proven" techniques you've been using to get ahead have been doing little more than creating extra work and may have been compromising your correct business behaviors.

Where such information will help you to understand the "why" of a rule, specific findings are presented from research in the areas of social psychology and organizational behavior. While theories in these areas are too general to be of any practical use, the results of specific research studies can be illuminating in developing your appreciation of the complexities you'll face in following the rules in a work environment. The appendices present additional general information relative to the organizational environment, social psychology, and group dynamics.

Even with your newfound knowledge and understanding, it won't be easy. Your full dedication and self-control will be needed to realize the business success benefits that this book can provide. The discipline you'll need would make a monk wince. Then again, monks have it easy; they don't have to fight it out with sharp, young tigers with top-school MBAs for a very few promotional opportunities. Once you aren't wasting your time on a lot of counterproductive nonsense, you'll have all the energy you need to stick with it if you want it badly enough.

For those of you with considerable business experience, this book will help you if it does nothing more than cause you to give careful thought and analysis to some of the almost unconscious ways you behave at work. You may be acting without conscious thought, but I can assure you that everyone is observing and evaluating your every move very consciously. You may discover that some of your "natural" behaviors are counterproductive to generating the image you must have to be maximally successful. Even the most accomplished and successful executive does a lot of seemingly minor things that irritate colleagues and hamper the effectiveness of employees. You can ignore these behaviors and their effects if you want ("I'm the boss, and I call the shots!"), but it's not wise. Few people are so high up the ladder that they can afford to throw away the opportunity to advance their careers by getting more from their organizations.

If you have little business experience or are just entering the job market, the rules in this book can have much more significance. It generally takes quite a few of the proverbial hard knocks (the consequences of serious strategic and tactical business errors) before a novice in the business world loses his or her "innocence." Most workers never do. There's no point in wasting several years or three or four good job opportunities (as countless thousands have done and will do) before you come to recognize what's really going on out there. If this book can speed up the process of getting you "on board," it will have served its purpose well.

Regardless of your specific situation and career ambitions, I am confident that the rules will, at the very least, improve your insight about what's going on at work. If you choose to try to follow the rules consistently, I'm sure that you'll get back more than you put out. Good luck!

2

Hard Talk About Some Hard Facts

This chapter presents ten hard facts about the real world of business. You may not like what I'm going to tell you, but I'm going to be straight with you at all times. First of all, you probably have a very distorted and unrealistic view of the business world. Don't feel too badly about it; you're not alone. Most people think they know what's going on around them at work. They think they've got their situations well under control. Most people are dead wrong. If you're viewing the world around you through an improper filter, you're going to be doing all sorts of things that will appear reasonable and logical but will be totally inappropriate to the way things really are. For example, let's suppose that you naively believe your organization will look out for your career development as long as you just do your job. If that were the case, you wouldn't be regularly scanning the classifieds to see what's available, you wouldn't be carefully reviewing opportunities for lateral moves within the organization, and you wouldn't be working hard to pump up the reputations of your boss, your department, and yourself. From your viewpoint, all of these activities would quite logically and reasonably appear to be superficial to "just doing a good job." Within the framework of such a distorted view, you would be correct. Within the real world of business, however, such an inaccurate viewpoint would result in circumstances that would seriously compromise the strongest career. Seeing through the correct filter provided by the ten hard facts in this chapter, you won't be tempted to wander down any false paths, you won't miss any significant information, and you won't waste your effort responding to false crises.

The rules that will be presented in Chapters 3 through 7 give specific guidelines for a wide variety of typical situations, problems, and opportunities with which you will have to deal successfully in order to reach your goals. Despite the wide range of situations covered, there will be times when you will encounter circumstances that are not covered by a specific rule. You'll be on your own then, just as you were before you happened upon this book. The hard facts which follow will enable you to determine the correct way to handle situations not covered by the rules.

Hard Fact 1: The universe is governed by the laws of probability. You are no exception.

The hard fact is this: You don't have as much control over your own destiny as you'd like to think you have. In fact, most of what happens to you is the result of forces you not only can't control but of which you probably aren't even aware. Consider the event of your own conception. You are the result of the union of one of your mother's egg cells with one of millions of sperm cells from your father. Your uniqueness results not only from your unique life experiences but also from the unique genetic composition of that chance union of one egg and one sperm. You've always seen yourself primarily as a product of your own efforts, haven't you? Well, it's time to face facts. Right from the start, your situation was more heavily influenced by probability than by your own efforts. It's not much different in business or life in general; your fate is influenced by a lot of factors over which you have no control.

Consider your present job. What if the first person to look at your résumé had been sickened by your selection of Executive Peach stationery and slipped it into the trash can? What if you hadn't read the classifieds on the only Sunday that your present job was advertised? What if the headhunter tried to call you on the one day your phone was out of order? How would you be doing if your boss was twice as stupid and mean as the worst boss you've ever worked for? Occurrences like these are totally out of your control, but any one of them would have critically influenced your current status. Yet, no matter what has happened to you up to this point, you've probably been assuming that it's more or less your own efforts that have molded your destiny. You take personal credit for causing the good things, while you attribute errors and failures to fate, chance, bad breaks, or someone else. You can't have it both ways. Both your successes and your failures are the result of both chance and your own efforts. Chance plays a larger part than most of us would like to admit.

All of us tend to think that we have control over what happens to us because we generally pay attention only to what we do and what happens as a result. We tend to assume a direct cause-and-effect relationship without considering all the thousands of other influences that had an impact. It's not comforting to think that we are objects of chance, adrift on the sea of probability. Our compensating, comforting belief that we are in control has been reinforced by the movies, literature, heroes, and legends of western civilization. The predominance of this view doesn't make it right; it only makes it more comforting. Consider the self-made millionaires whom all aspiring successes envy. Would they have had the drive to succeed if they had been born in a small Third World village? Would they have turned into towering capitalists if they had been working in the fields at the age of ten instead of attending boarding schools? Probably not. Yet these individuals and most observers readily attribute their successes to the individuals' drive and intelligence. While their own actions were vital to their success, their efforts had a very small effect when compared to the myriad of other influences that shaped their situations.

Since many of the factors that influence a situation are out of our control or beyond our notice, we must work triply hard to influence the few factors on which we can have an impact. The probabilistic view of the world doesn't mean that you have no control and can therefore abrogate responsibility for your fate. If you were to give up and simply trust your fate to destiny, you'd be letting the unknown factors have full sway. Some of the time you'd luck out, and some of the time you'd lose out. But you'd very seldom come out ahead of the people who were working hard on every available item under their control. The presence of so many unknown factors means that you have to work like a dervish so that you'll come out on top after the positive and negative uncontrollable factors have had their effects on your destiny.

Hard Fact 2: Fairness and justice are abstract concepts that are not an inherent part of nature.

Life as we know it reached its current state as the result of thousands of minor evolutionary changes superimposed on countless previous changes. Every life form on this planet exists today in its present form only because that form could survive long enough to spawn the next generation. Thousands of species have perished because their forms weren't efficient enough at reproduction to offset deaths from disease, predators, climate changes, and so on. We are animals, the product of random genetic mutations and evolution. Our brains and bodies and the social organization and behaviors they permit are the products of random changes that enable us to reproduce fast enough so that we don't die out. Evolution does not provide for justice and fairness, only survival for what works. Hoping for justice and fairness out of frustration will not help.

When businesspeople say, "It's a jungle out there!" they are more right than they know but for a different reason than they think. It's not a jungle because it's rough and difficult. It's a jungle because there is no justice and fairness.

Hard Fact 3: You're really not too important in the scope of things.

Right now, at this very moment, there are millions of hard-working people who have fears and hopes just like yours. In fact, there are millions of lazy incompetents who also have the same hopes and fears that you have and who don't even realize that they're less qualified for success. Yet each one of these millions feels that he or she is just as special and unique and deserving as you think you are. Even famous historical figures are known mainly for a few public acts that tell us little about their internal struggles, hopes, and dreams.

Face it, almost everybody lives and dies without any great impact on history or events. And even if you do make some important contributions, if you disappeared tomorrow, do you think the place where you work would just fold up? Would they close the bowling alley and the racquetball club just because you wouldn't be coming anymore? You get the point. As nice as you are, there are thousands of other people who are just as nice, as charming, and as special as you think you are. So what's the big deal about making it in business? Do you really believe that you can do something so great that nobody else could do it? Do you think that if you don't do it, it won't get done? There are thousands of people who can match your "unique" contributions step for step, so don't put a lot of unnecessary pressure on yourself. Are you working for yourself, for your spouse, for your family? If it isn't for your personal achievement and satisfaction here and now, don't do it.

All of us living now will be dead in eighty years at the outside. A whole new group of people will be living in our houses, driving on our roads, and working in our offices. They won't think about us, and they won't care about what we did. You are probably not here to fulfill a crowning destiny and lead humanity to the millennium. So take it easy on yourself. Relax a little. The pressure is off. You've got nothing to prove and nobody to prove it to except yourself.

Hard Fact 4: You've got to take the long, slow road to success.

Forget the big play. Forget the last-second touchdown. Forget the rags-to-riches stories. They are the stuff of romantic legends. What you must have to succeed in business is a long series of small, low-profile victories, not a few isolated, major triumphs. Who ever heard of Dwight Eisenhower before World War II? He worked his way up the ladder by following the rules every day; no major triumphs, just small, repeated, consistent, low-profile victories within the system day after day. He wasn't even a great strategic or tactical general, but he had enough consistent, day-to-day "victories" to end up as the president of the United States. The CEO of IBM did not get to the top by one daring play of making a desperate lunge at a long-shot. The CEO got there by carefully playing the high-probability odds over the long run, by consistently obeying the rules, and by taking only a very few carefully calculated risks at rule breaking. You must do the same if you wish to get to the top. The big play is dangerous and ineffective.

Our preoccupation with the big play is the result of western civilization's philosophical emphasis upon heroic fantasies that portray incredible individual feats of courage and strength as the ideal. We are constantly bombarded by epics in which a single act of personal initiative is sufficient to transform impending doom into instant, complete, and total victory. The problem with this is that the heroes of these stories are always people who win by taking incredible risks that defy all odds. Have you ever seen John Wayne portray a reticent accountant who was afraid to argue with his boss? Does Clint Eastwood portray a policeman who keeps his mouth shut and his gun holstered as he studies for the next promotion exam? Of course not. Such stories wouldn't be exciting; they wouldn't appeal to our emotional needs.

Admit it. Your fantasies of yourself always involve incredible, unexpected displays of power and skill that instantly turn a desperate situation into a glorious and acclaimed triumph. Such fantasies are a healthy outlet for occasional use. But don't let them distort your view of the real world. For every successful big play, there are dozens of miserable failures. Taking big chances just doesn't work out.

You'll soon learn why it's career suicide to be too aggressive at work. Yet we've been led to believe that there's a place in business for the type of outrageous behavior the heroic legends present. The plain, unromantic, unexciting truth is that there are countless mealy-mouthed, blow-with-the-wind people out there who make it to the top. And there are many aggressive, outrageous, and bold people who make it only because they carefully and tightly hide their true colors at work. There are few Dirty Harry types who become successful by acting out their big-play instincts in real life. Don't let your emotional need for a little excitement distort your evaluation of how often exceptions to the rules work out.

Success over the long haul requires not only the abandonment of your childlike attachment for big plays but something even more difficult: day-to-day, hour-to-hour, and minute-to-minute consistency in following the rules. You must follow the rules every second and in every circumstance. This means no exceptions. In the worst case, your entire career with an organization could be summarily destroyed by one mistake. At the very least, a single rule violation could cause repercussions that could ruin months of careful rule following. Since you'll get few, if any, chances to make dramatic positive impressions, you can't afford to make any negative ones, no matter how little. It's just too hard to recover.

Otherwise cautious achievers are sometimes tempted to disobey the rules and take reckless chances when they are desperately attempting to make up ground after a setback. This is always a serious tactical and strategic error. When you have suffered a setback, your finely honed business skills are at their worst. More critically, your wounded pride and ambition will distort your analysis of your chances of pulling off a risky maneuver. Misguided managers have actually been known to point out obvious and serious flaws in their bosses' business plans as they tried to make up for earlier errors. After serious setbacks, others have done such foolish things as trying to increase company profits by pointing out the folly of existing policies. It's frightening what some people will do when they get desperate. Hang in there; the long-term odds will work for you if you play long enough. It isn't going to go your way all the time; you know that in advance. So don't get upset and discouraged when the inevitable and expected setbacks occur. Remember that long-term success is your goal. A few minor or even major defeats do not mean you will lose the war.

It's just as important not to overreact to your successes. When things start to go right, we're all tempted to start thinking that we're special and that things are working out only because we're so wonderful. If you allow this to happen, you'll soon start to think you can win with the big play. Then you'll find out how special you are to the gods of probability. Even the lions die; it's a jungle out there.

Hard Fact 5: Your "natural" inclinations and instincts are dangerous to your career.

There are thousands of people who do good work but will never get anywhere. You know who they are. They're often described by comments such as, "Frank does a good job, but he's just not executive material," or, "Yes, Sally can sure pump out that work, and she's really got that department organized, but she's just not the general manager type." What Frank and Sally are perceived to lack is the image of a successful businessperson as their organizations view such people. Whether they actually are executive timber or not is immaterial. If others perceive a lack, the careers of Sally and Frank are in trouble.

Sally and Frank aren't deliberately trying to ruin their careers. They're working hard to present what they believe will work: their natural, pleasant, gifted selves. That's their problem; they're simply doing what comes naturally. Their demeanor at work is a slightly more formal and better-dressed performance of the typical social behaviors they perform when they are at home or out with friends. They are behaving naturally and according to the common-sense dictates and values that society and their parents taught them. Such "natural" behaviors are bad news for any career.

Our social repertoire is the result of eons of evolution. We are the descendants of a long line of social primates. Most primates are social animals; we are no different. Our need for social contact with others of our species evolved over hundreds of thousands of years. With primitive subhumanoids, group cooperation was absolutely essential. If an individual became separated from the group, death soon followed. We are social today because social subhumanoids managed to survive better than those who were not.

One result of this inbred social structure is that our young are born totally helpless and must be protected and cared for over a period of many years. This requires some sort of family or group unit for protection. The closeness of the group results in and reinforces the development of social bonds, individuals' needs for them, and the skills to support and obtain them. The resulting social structures form quite naturally and are very complex. The security and comfort that social bonds provide are very important to our health and survival as individuals. Babies who do not receive enough social contact in the form of handling and attention fail to thrive, and many even die. Children who don't experience normal home environments tend to have problems later on with social interactions and relationships. Adults who live alone, outside a close relationship, tend to get sick more often and, as a group, die at an earlier age. Our needs to be social are a stronger force in our lives than our intellects. While we must satisfy these inbred and reinforced needs for social contact in order to remain physically and mentally healthy, work is not the place to do it.

The problem is that our social tendencies are the result of an evolutionary process that was operating in a life-or-death environment. Despite some executives' protestations to the contrary, things are not that desperate in today's business world. People switch from job to job without any dire (and sometimes with favorable) consequences. Few people believe that their very existence is tied to the fate of the work group. In contrast to the close, interdependent social environment in which our social behaviors evolved, the social environment of modern business is loose, short-term (switching jobs is a routine practice), non-life-threatening, and not intensely interdependent. Our natural tendencies are not appropriate in today's work environment. Behaving according to the dictates of social tendencies that were developed to deal with survival in a hostile environment will cause you to behave in ways that will be counterproductive for your career.

One specific area in which natural reactions can get you in a lot of trouble is that of first impressions. A lot of people swear by their first impressions and use them as the primary basis for many of their decisions. This is a serious mistake. Your first impression of anything is an involuntary emotional response over which you have little control. For example, you may occasionally take an instant liking to someone you are meeting for the first time. If you were to give it some thought, you'd probably discover that the person looked, behaved, or spoke a little like a favorite relative or a fondly remembered work associate. These types of unconscious and involuntary responses can lead you into all sorts of trouble if you don't control them. One way to avoid serious errors is to take your time in all interactions. Practice a strategy of letting things develop for a few minutes in a new situation so that you can respond after your emotional reaction has subsided. If you find yourself reacting emotionally in an inappropriate manner (which is any unplanned emotional reaction at work) and you don't understand why, hold off on any action for a while and give it some thought. You'll probably discover the real reason for your reaction after a little reflection. Once you understand the basis for a specific emotional reaction, you'll be less likely to overreact the next time.

Hard Fact 6: Technical job skills are a minor consideration compared to the image you project.

All you've got to do is read the typical job advertisement or position description and you'd think that technical skills, educational degrees, and years of experience are all you need to get a job and eventually become a successful businessperson. This notion is total nonsense. The reason for the emphasis on degrees, years of experience, and the like is that such items are easily quantifiable. It makes personnel officers and executives feel like they're being scientific when they're able to state categorically that the job can only be done by "an MBA (from a top school, of course), with seven to nine years of experience, and two to three years of experience in nondeterministic financial modeling." Do they really think they can be precise enough to differentiate between the amount of actual technical experience on two persons' résumés, one showing five years on the job and the other with seven? They can't. The person with "only" five years of experience may have been doing ten projects at once in a high-pressure environment with exacting standards and demanding clients. The other may have been poking along on one project at a time for the entire seven years and messing everything up in the process. But the personnel officers and hiring managers want to appear quantitative, so they start specifying and counting years. Why is a top-school MBA so magical that almost every other ad either demands it outright or says that it's preferred? There's no magic—just a lot of executives playing the at-work variant of keeping up with the Joneses. Technical qualifications, degrees, and credentials are labels, and we're a label-conscious society in business just as much as in our clothing preferences.

This emphasis on job skills as the major crux of attention would not be a problem if it remained in the executive suite and personnel departments only. It is easy enough to go out and get an MBA from some night school that specializes in pumping them out. Such a degree will satisfy 99 percent of the educational requirements of most job descriptions and advertisements calling for an MBA. Unfortunately, the technical skill virus has spread into all corners of the business world and has infected everyone. The continuing and growing emphasis on job skills, MBA and other degrees, professional conferences, and professional certifications in specialties has brainwashed many people into erroneously believing that the battle up the corporate ladder is fought with sheepskins and framed certificates. Nothing could be further from the truth. In actual fact, the rush to acquire badges of technical skills has created a situation in which many workers ignore areas that are more basic and critical to business success. As a result, you can go to any number of meetings with certified, degreed, and technically qualified people and find that nobody knows the first thing about optimizing employee productivity (as opposed to talking about it), properly managing the boss, business etiquette and courtesy, and so on. Not only do they think it's not important, but a lot of them don't even know that these types of factors are much more critical than technical job skills. You'll find that these brainwashed individuals will see nothing wrong with badgering and arguing with their bosses day in and day out, failing to maintain visibility and contact with their employees, and perhaps even openly expressing doubts about the organization's goals. After all, they reason, they know what they're doing technically, so it must be OK, right? Wrong.

Don't fall prey to the tendency to view hard technical skills as the most important aspect of your job. Once you have the basic credentials required to get the job or move up to the level you are seeking, concentrate instead on cultivating the total package you present to everyone in the work environment. You can do that by following the rules.

Hard Fact 7: Your greatest obstacles to success are your own expectations, fears, and insecurities.

The hardest of the hard facts to face is that we are our own greatest obstacle to getting where we want to go. Buried deep within our psyches are the fears, doubts, and insecurities that our parents and society installed in us when we were children. These buried inadequacies sometimes prevent us from giving our best, and, often, they prevent us from even trying. You can't do a total remodeling job on your personality at this late stage in your life, but you can perform some significant modifications. The first step in any type of change is awareness of the many things within you that influence your behaviors but of which you aren't always aware.

You can't afford to view yourself as any less significant than anyone else. If you do, you'll delay action because you'll be convinced that your chances are poor. Believe me, everyone has the same fears and insecurities that you have. Sometimes it seems as if everyone else is more self-assured, more composed, and more ''together'' than you feel. Inside, you wonder if you're ever going to get to the point where you truly feel ''grown up.'' You probably won't; you'll just get used to it. Relax. Everybody feels the same way; we all have the same fears and doubts. The only difference between you and others is that some of them may be better actors in public and better liars to themselves in private. Clergy, presidents, parents, butchers, bakers, candlestick makers, and executives are no different. Don't waste your energy worrying about how you stack up; we're all in the same boat.

The great equalizer among people is early childhood experience. The rough framework of your personality was formed at a very early age. Your basic moral sense, your attitudes about right and wrong, your view of other people's rights, your internal emotional reactions to people and things, and the way you approach a problem were established before you learned to drive. Unknowingly, your parents were teaching you to act and think like a winner, loser, tryer, resigner, and so on. Your later experiences were perceived in ways that would fit the framework that your parents and other influences installed in you. By following their often unspoken, almost certainly not planned, and unconscious instructions, you earned your kisses and cookies and gradually adopted many of their attitudes and behaviors, known as scripts. While there is a wide variety of child-rearing orientations in western civilization, there is an even more amazing similarity. The result is that almost everyone comes away with a remarkably similar bag of insecurities, fears, and doubts. Even the assortment of scripts is not as diverse as you'd expect.

Do not underestimate the power of scripts taught in early childhood to influence behavior. As an extreme but illuminating example, consider the behavior of child molesters, wife beaters, and other types of violent people. Upon investigation, it turns out that almost all of the persons who exhibit these types of behaviors were themselves long-term victims of the same abuses when they were young. They learned the scripts for child abuse, wife beating, and so on, by observing it and/or being subjected to it at home. This makes it a little easier to understand why abused wives sometimes tolerate such treatment for years and years and why abused children frequently become child abusers themselves. To these poor victims, such behavior represented normal activity in their parents' homes. Learned while they were children, such scripts are deeply ingrained and cannot be easily changed.

All of us have had more subtle but equally powerful scripts forced upon us by parents and teachers when we were young. Such scripts can be changed once you recognize them and want to change them, but it isn't easy. You can do it if you work at it. You can't control a lot of the factors that affect your life, but you can free yourself to approach your challenges in your own unique style. So take a good, hard look at some of the bad things that keep happening to you. Then think back to the way your parents used to act, some of the values that were important to them, things they would dwell on, and the general view of the world that they held when you were young. You'll probably discover that quite a lot of your behavior is tied to the scripts that they taught you. Once you consciously recognize some of your mistakes as the result of scripts, you can start to change them if you desire (not all scripts are bad; some are excellent).

Hard Fact 8: The business world is a confused and chaotic mess.

It's no different from any other aspect of life. The business world is a complex, chaotic, and unpredictable maelstrom that lumbers along without any systematic planning and only rarely with any rational judgment. Neither look for nor expect order and efficiency. There is none. Many novices in the business world and almost all academians are impressed with the towering skyscrapers, paneled boardrooms, glossy corporate reports, expensive clothes, and costly attaché cases. They see these things and assume that the decision-making and operational systems are just as towering, paneled, and glossy. Forget it; every organization in the business world is just as inefficient and disorganized as the most confused and inept small business you've ever seen. You see the confusion, stupidity, waste, corruption, pettiness, and incompetence where you work, but you may think it's different in other companies and business in general. It's not; it looks bigger, better-dressed, glossier, and more paneled, but it's the same. I've worked in, consulted with, and/or managed companies that earned from $250,000 to $350,000,000 per year. I've worked in industries ranging from high-tech software and engineering firms to industrial bakeries to classified government research. There are the same people, the same procedures, the same hassles, and (luckily for you) the same opportunity to apply the rules in every organization in the world.

The stated purpose of business in a capitalistic society is to accumulate and utilize profits for the benefit of the investors. Very few companies allow this minor consideration to interfere with the empire building and ego aggrandizement of managers and executives. Very few business decisions are free from the overpowering influence of the emotional needs of those involved. Every year, hundreds of companies lose billions of dollars because they pursue patently idiotic objectives set by top managers and executives. Railroads go bankrupt, banks fail, and manufacturers lose hundreds of millions because executives will not subrogate their personal biases and ambitions to more objective considerations. It's always been this way, and it always will be. Of course, great successes sometimes occur as a result of executives' personal prejudices, beliefs, hunches, and pet projects. Unfortunately, most executives don't have superior long-term instincts in these areas any more than most nonexecutives do; it's just that they're in a position to see that their hunches get tried. The result is thousands of bad decisions every day. Some are small and made by a single person. Businesses are created and largely operate to satisfy personal needs and egos. Profits are an incidental occurrence.

Hard Fact 9: Don't expect much satisfaction from a job.

If you do, you will be sorely disappointed. You have unique requirements for affection, self-esteem, excitement, and achievement that are different from everybody else's. No one else has your unique combination of genes, upbringing, and experience. Yet there are thousands of people who are working in the same type of job that you have, facing the same assortment of problems, challenges, coworkers, and frustrations. Each person will be satisfied to a different degree with the job, depending upon the unique dimensions of their personalities, expectations, and past history. Your specific needs cannot possibly be satisfied by an off-the-shelf job. As a result, most people are jammed into ill-fitting jobs that have no actual relationship to their unique skills, assets, and needs. One specific job has less chance of meeting your unique needs than one universal cut of suit would fit everyone; personalities differ a lot more than body dimensions.

Worse yet, the satisfaction of your unique needs requires some degree of childlike behavior on your part, some degree of vulnerability, and quite a bit of candor and sincerity. The display of these types of behaviors at work is a serious violation of almost every other rule in this book. After all, candor and sincerity are natural social behaviors. As such, they are bad news at work. Avoid them at all costs unless you work with a group of subhumanoids who are struggling to survive in a primitive environment. Devote a considerable amount of attention toward making sure that you are satisfying your needs for relationships, love, and excitement after working hours. Off the job, you can afford to be more natural as you are seeking to establish and build relationships based on trust, love, friendship, and common commitments. Your relationships at work must be based only on those behaviors that will create the best image possible. Actual candor, sincerity, trust, love, and shared intimacies will only create trouble at work. Keep them in your private life. Your career will benefit, and you'll end up with a higher quality of interpersonal relationships.

Even if you're looking for a much more limited type of satisfaction—the old-fashioned pat on the back for a job well done—you're going to come up short most of the time. When you wonder "Where's my thanks?" you'd better be prepared to provide your own. Each of the people at work has a lot of other things to worry about, the least of which is their job and your small part of that world. About the last item on their agenda is seeing that you get enough strokes. They are dying a thousand deaths with their own internal fears and hopes and dreams, and you want them to pat you on the back? Don't count on it. In fact, if you find that you're constantly seeking a lot of strokes and attention as a payoff for your work, it probably means that you aren't doing what you really want to do. If you're not committed to waging a serious, long-term battle to be a business success, you'll constantly be seeking assurances from others that you're doing the right thing. Nobody can give you enough of that type of reassurance to make it worth the suffering.

Hard Fact 10: There are a lot of mean, nasty, stupid people out there who are very dangerous to your career.

There are many bad people in the world. Some of these bad people go to work every day in offices like yours. It is a well-established fact of social dynamics that geographical proximity leads to increased liking. This social phenomenon probably had survival value in primitive societies. Such a natural social dynamic has a tremendous negative survival value for your career. Be aware that there are all sorts of people who delight in causing hurt and suffering to people and careers as an end in itself. Do not trust someone and drop your guard just because they happen to have a job where you work.

The mean and nasty people are far outnumbered by hordes who are marginally intelligent and noncreative. Don't be misled by TV, movies, and the general media into believing that intelligence and creativity are universally admired and respected. No one will say that he or she is 100 percent behind stupidity and ignorance, but those who are don't like anyone who is more intelligent and gifted than they are. For a lot of people, this means that they don't like almost everyone. These people are frustrated and anxious as they contemplate their sorry lot in life. They know they're not going anywhere, and they know everyone else knows it. Their prospects are much more limited than yours; you still hope that you'll make it (or you wouldn't be reading this book). They have no more hope. Put yourself in their shoes for a minute. How do you think you'd feel if you knew—really knew—you'd never go any farther than you are now? Well, not many people will admit it, but they know the race is over for them. They know that all they can do is watch everyone else run by. How do you explain to your family, spouse, friends, and yourself that you're a failure and you know that you can't change it? It's rough to deal with. Fortunately for the rest of us, most of these people are content to live out their lives of quiet desperation without causing a lot of trouble. They just want to be left alone and not be reminded of their plight any more than is absolutely necessary. You are advised to let sleeping failures lie. If you rub it in and force them to have to deal with their plight, you risk serious problems. While they may not have the equipment to succeed, they have all the tools they need (a mouth and friends who will listen) to seriously impede the upward movement of the career of ''some show-off.'' Do the smart thing and leave these poor wretches alone. It will help your career, and it's an act of compassion as well. (There's nothing wrong with being nice at work if it can't hurt you.) Any unnecessary displays of intelligence and creativity at work are dangerous. Keep them out of sight, and use them only to follow the rules.

Even if the people where you work are reasonably decent and intelligent, they can't be trusted. People aren't at their best at work. Most of them are there not because they love it but because they have no choice. Believe this and consider the consequences of it. Routine studies repeatedly demonstrate that lots of people can't stand their jobs. If none of us had to work, we probably wouldn't sit around all the time but we certainly wouldn't interrupt whatever we were doing to go to management meetings or give performance reviews. Skiing, woodworking, painting, fishing, gardening, reading novels, and so on, would be our work activities. Most people have dozens of things they would rather do instead of going to work. And the typical job provides almost none of the things people want most from work: challenge, a sense of achievement, a feeling of being involved and valued, and recognition for a task well done. Yet almost all of us are forced by recurring hunger pangs and a reluctance to sleep in the rain to drag ourselves to some boring, mundane job day after day and year after year. The consequence is that people come to work with a lot of frustration, anger, and disappointment. Like caged tigers, they are limited to pacing back and forth, forced to try to control their energy and emotions as they perceive that the world is going by without them. Their frustrations and hostilities are on hair triggers. They are dangerous. You'd never dream of walking into a tiger's cage without a whip and chair. Well, it's no safer for you to walk your career into the office every day. Since you have no choice, watch the tigers very carefully. The jungle floor is carpeted with the bones of careers whose owners let down their guards.

3

Rules for Understanding Organizations and Dealing with Executives

This chapter presents rules that will help you to anticipate, understand, and deal with the behavior of organizations and executives. Organizations and executives generate a lot of behaviors and rituals that might appear to be silly, meaningless, or stupid to an independent outside observer. From your position within the organization, you can't afford to adopt that viewpoint. Your outlook must be dependent, career-oriented, and subjective. This means that you must treat every little bit of executive and organizational nonsense as the deadly serious threats to your career that they can be if not handled correctly. Every organizational ritual and executive mannerism is very significant to the organization. You must respect or emulate these behaviors and rituals if you want to be successful. It is critically important for you to understand what these behaviors are, why they occur, and why they persist despite what appear to be attempts on the part of individuals and the organizations themselves to change them. Whether you work as a nurse in a hospital, as a management trainee in a factory, or as a middle manager in a bank, you'll see that organizations and executives display remarkably consistent behavior. The only thing that really changes from industry to industry is the jargon and the stationery; the social and group dynamics are identical. The rules in this chapter will provide you with guidelines for dealing successfully with executives and coexisting in organizations across the entire spectrum of industries and work environments.

Rule 1: Expect each organization to play a different version of the game.

The rules are universally applicable. In any organization, their consistent use will significantly increase your probability of long-term success. This is because every organization is peopled with the same types of human egos, personality needs, fears, and anxieties. However, each organization has a unique style that emphasizes some social rituals more and others less. For example, in some organizations it is mandatory for everyone to appear to be happy and to work together. These organizations place a primary emphasis on company rituals, company jargon, expressed feelings of togetherness, and sometimes even group calisthenics in tune to the company song at their desks. Employment interviews at these organizations are a combination of the confessional and the positive-thinking pep rally. The employees smile a lot as they talk about how great their organization is, how great the employees are, how great the management is, and so forth. Of course, such an extreme approach is just as ridiculous as the more widespread myth that each manager in an organization is an independent warrior out to prove himself or herself as worthy on the business field of honor. If you want to succeed in any organization, you have to appear to play by their rules.

The bottom line is that you must always behave as if you ardently believe in the currently popular social rituals and propaganda line. Let's suppose that ABC Company operates on a slight variant of Rule 51, which is that it's OK to give the appearance of arguing a little with the boss. By allowing employees to give the appearance of arguing with them, the management of ABC Company is able to support its fantasy that things are laid back and participative and that "the employees aren't afraid to come in here and tell us how they feel." This organizational ritual serves a useful purpose for the executives of ABC Company (reduction of guilt over their failure to do anything meaningful to move ABC Company into the twentieth century of business practices), and they foster it. Within ABC Company, good rule following would require you to play the ABC Company version of Rule 51: Give the appearance of arguing a little, but don't actually argue. If you were to misread the situation and break Rule 51 outright by really arguing, you'd be in big trouble. For example:

Fred: "Well, J.B., I've looked over your plan for the new product rollout, and I'm not sure I completely understand the reason for...."

This represents a little arguing with the boss. Actually, Fred thinks the whole idea is idiotic, but he just wants to play the game by pretending not to agree completely.

J.B.: "I'm glad you asked, Fred. Let me explain my thinking on that...."

This means that J.B. is glad that Fred is giving him an opportunity to "mentor" him and at the same time demonstrate that J.B. is entirely open to criticism. At this point, Fred will have argued a "little" and satisfied the rules of the game as they're played at ABC Company. Now, let's suppose Fred wasn't lucky enough to have read this book and continued to argue after J.B. had finished the lecture.

Fred: "Well, I still think we're making a big mistake here, J.B. XYZ Industries tried this last year and lost out big."

Now Fred has really done it. He is arguing in substance and not just form. He is breaking Rule 51 and will pay the horrible price.

J.B.: "Look, Fred, our situation is different, but it's clear that you just don't have enough experience to see it. I'd love to explain it to you, but I've got a meeting. Maybe we can talk tomorrow."

What the boss really means is that he now realizes that Fred is not the bright person everyone thought he was. Fred broke an unspoken but universal rule because he did not accurately interpret the style of rule playing that takes place at ABC Company. Fred is in trouble and will stay there until he can work his way out by careful rule following during future encounters with J.B. It will take him many weeks. Make sure that you understand exactly what style of rule following is considered proper in your organization. If you are new to your organization, play it safe and observe all of the rules to the absolute letter; they represent the most conservative and safest course of action. Once you have learned the nuances of a particular organization's style, you can modify the rules to match its unique expectations more closely. Prior to that point, you cannot afford to take the risk of modifying a rule. The small added benefit you might obtain is far outweighed by the career dangers that a small miscalculation could bring.

Rule 2: Do not expect organizations to behave as if they have consciences or morals.

An organization is composed of people. Take away the people and the organization disappears. As the character and personalities of the organization's people change, so does the behavior of the organization itself. Organizations may seem like entities in and of themselves, but they are not. You cannot deal with an organization; you must deal with the people. The organization will not take care of you, protect you from injustice, or help you in time of need any more than the people themselves would. In fact, organizations demonstrate less compassion than individuals; there is always a frustrated and unhappy person standing by to cite procedures and regulations in order to thwart an attempted act of compassion by someone else who has a little consideration. They're the ones who tell some poor soul, "I'd personally love to let you take two days of the forty vacation days you've accrued (by slaving without a day off for four years) so you can fly back to your mother's funeral, but policy is policy. You didn't have your request in five days in advance. I'm sorry."

Organizations foster this type of behavior when they focus on processes rather than results. You've seen them, and you've worked for them. They're the companies where it doesn't matter how much you sell or how much service you give the customers; the important thing is to fill out all the forms right and never do anything that isn't 100 percent by the book even if it's an emergency. What has happened in these companies is that less than gifted employees have established a company culture where the day-to-day objectives don't include profits, results, or efficiency. The only thing they worry about is the process itself, not the results. Once that happens, protecting the processes becomes more important than the customers, the work, and the employees. Employees in such organizations quickly lose their motivation to do anything more than blindly enforce and follow policies. In such an environment, compassion and consideration, not to mention creativity and performance, are quickly stifled. To believe that "I'm not worried about my job, the company would never lay off someone with twenty-eight years and only two years to go before pension" is folly. If a new president takes over and decides to cut costs mercilessly, there are going to be a lot of sixty-three-year-old workers with twenty-eight years in who will be trying to avoid starvation by living on Social Security. So much for an organization's conscience. Don't trust it; it isn't there.

Rule 3: Always behave as if you are unflinchingly loyal to the organization and as if you believe that the organization feels the same way about you.

Loyalty is one of those things everyone talks a lot about but nobody really does much about. For example, everyone talks about loyalty to their country, but then they cheat like crazy on their taxes. Loyalty in business is pretty much the same thing; there's a lot of talk, but that's about all. Such a situation is good news for you because it's a lot easier to talk a loyal tune than it is to act loyal.

An organization pays its members to perform certain activities. If an employee doesn't perform the expected activities to the organization's satisfaction, the organization will eventually come to the conclusion that it's not getting its money's worth and will terminate the employee. To the organization, it's a clearcut case of classic capitalistic supply and demand. Loyalty to the employee will not enter into the picture. Years of service, past contributions, sacrifices of family life, and even personal health will not be considered. At the same time as they are firing people and laying them off, organizations are continually trumpeting their undying loyalty to employees in press releases and annual reports. Loyalty to the employee is a fiction, but it's imperative for you always to generate and support talk about how the organization treats its employees with loyalty.

Loyalty from the employees to the organization is much the same thing. Nobody really demonstrates it, but everybody talks about it a lot. It's interesting that in a capitalistic society organizations behave as if employees owe them more than hard work for their wages. This, of course, is nonsense. It's irrational to expect such an additional unpaid and unreciprocated service from employees, but they do expect it. The reason for this emphasis on loyalty is as follows. Many organization members find comfort in the superstitious belief that the organization is an independent entity with a paternalistic personality. These members cannot or do not want to face the fears and insecurities of life as individuals on their own. They need to feel as if something greater is behind them. When someone demonstrates disloyal behavior, their belief system is threatened. The result is an increase in the anxiety level of the "believers." Rather than dealing with their own feelings, the believers will attack the person who stirs up their fears.

In order to deal successfully with this phenomenon, you must learn how to demonstrate convincing bowing and scraping behaviors before the organizational deity. Fortunately, most of the expected behavior is just talk. You and everyone else can still switch jobs with impunity and be viewed as loyal by both the old and the new organization as long as you talk a good game.

Rule 4: Do not attempt to force changes upon an organization.

Organizations abhor change. And the bigger they get, the more they abhor it. All people like routine. It's comforting to have familiar things around us, because the familiarity reduces the amount of new information processing we must do from moment to moment.

The usual, expected routine is easy and nonthreatening. There is no new information to process, and what worked yesterday will probably work tomorrow and next week. When change is in the wind, the non-adventurers (almost everyone) will resist it with all of their considerable inertia. They've been protecting the processes instead of doing real work for so long that they've forgotten how to do real work (creative approaches that increase effectiveness). To avoid facing this problem, they resist. The more of them there are, the greater the inertia and resistance. Each of them will resist change to the extent that he or she is threatened. That's why it's harder to change things in a larger organization; you've got hundreds of little gears and cogs freezing up on you instead of three or four. Only dire threats to the organization can act to loosen this resistance, and then only a little. The sad fact is that almost no company can significantly change its company culture. Only dire and acute threats to the very survival of the organization have any chance of motivating comprehensive and lasting changes. When big changes do take place, they occur because great numbers of new employees and managers move in, a lot of dead wood is tossed out, and the very fabric of the company changes. Even then, most of the old employees who remain continue to operate as usual (although there may be fewer of them). If organizations can't change even in response to dire threats to their own existence, how much real change do you think you can effect? Do not waste your time and damage your image by trying to introduce changes.

While the above may make it appear as if change in an organization is impossible, take heart; organizations do change a lot. The problem is that the pace of the change is glacial and cannot be increased by pushing from within on the part of a few aggressive managers. It will occur at a rate dictated by the style of the organization and by pressures imposed upon the organization by society and the marketplace. Such changes almost always occur at a pace that is too slow to notice, much too slow to suit the career needs of an aggressive, aspiring employee. If you find that you require significant changes in your organization in order to "strut your stuff," you've got a big problem.

The significance of this situation is that if you want change (that is, if you need change for career purposes), you can either sit and wait for the organization to evolve as a result of external pressures or you can seek a different organization whose current structure may be more conducive to your purposes. Those are the only two choices you have; you'll never be able to change the organization fast enough to suit your own rapidly evolving career needs. If you try to push an organization toward change faster than its natural rate, you'll only succeed in creating one change: You'll open up your job slot for someone else.

Rule 5: Do not expect the systems of an organization to function smoothly.

It's almost a miracle that they work at all. At first glance, any moderately successful organization appears to be a smoothly functioning machine. Work appears to be getting done, people are attending meetings (which means that no work is getting done), memos go out, and everybody is dressed like a businessperson. In successful organizations there appears to be a smooth hush of earnest business activity, but don't count on it. An organization's systems evolve in a haphazard manner, as different people put in parts to satisfy their personality needs, fears, and even in some rare cases their rational expert opinion of the most cost-effective approach. Do not expect these systems to work very well.

Indicative of this sorry (but natural and inevitable) condition are the gut-wrenching reorganizations that many companies go through as often as every year. The avowed reason for these reorganizations, to hear the executives tell it, is to "shake things up and keep people hopping." If things aren't working, it makes sense to change them. The problem is that if things are so bad that everything has to be reorganized every year or so, you have to wonder if the executives are doing their jobs in the first place. Most of the time they're not. Constant reorganizations merely represent inept and feverish attempts to stumble upon a smaller mess than the current one. That such things occur regularly in most organizations is ample evidence that things don't evolve in a smooth, logical, and rational manner. On the other hand, you must recognize and believe that an organization's systems are cherished parts of the organization. Whether they actually work well or not is always a very minor consideration. Don't expect things to work very well, and don't express your disappointment when the inevitable messes occur. Most of all, don't risk your success by attempting to change systems for purely performance and/or cost-effectiveness reasons.

Rule 6: Talk a lot about how organizations value their people, but do not expect them to do it.

Make no mistake about it; people are the most important part of any organization—they *are* the organization. Good people make more difference than market share, a good cash position, or an aggressive management team. Organizations always mouth these words, but they don't believe them (except when executives are talking about themselves and attempting to justify additional bonuses or perquisites). The book *In Search of Excellence* presents in detail some of the strategies used by a number of successful organizations to develop and effectively utilize their personnel. If your organization isn't operating with these or similar strategies now, the chances are 100,000 to 1 that they won't be. Most organizations do not use these strategies because they are difficult to administer. Since most executives and managers want to do as little work as possible, they are content to trade potential productivity increases (which nobody sees as a loss) for less work in the present. A further reason for the relative lack of cost-effective employee development in business is that most managers either are not comfortable with such programs or they are, quite simply, too stupid to manage them properly.

Place no faith in an organization's ability or resolve to value its personnel or its contentions that it does value them unless there is extremely strong evidence to the contrary. If you wish to test the waters in any organization, simply investigate the relative difficulties of trying to buy another typewriter or desktop computer with those of trying to add another person. You'll probably find that it's a lot easier to justify the added person even though the person's first-year salary will far exceed the equipment cost. I worked in one high-tech organization in which the company president had to get the chairman of the board's signature for every purchase over $1,000. Yet department heads were free to hire as many people as they could justify. The result: It took months to get furniture, but you could quickly hire people to sit in empty offices. Even in tough economic times, it's relatively easy to add people because the organization knows it can get rid of them much more easily than it can cost-effectively dispose of equipment. Look about your organization and observe how many secretaries become managers and executives—not many, I'm sure. That type of progression would indicate a sincere concern on the part of the organization for the self-fulfillment of its people (as well as smart, long-term management development planning). Few companies do it.

In order to live with this reality, you must appear to believe that the organization values its people, but you must never push too hard for things such as job enrichment, better benefits, or more money for top performers. Don't push even if you know that such things would increase productivity and result in a better profit margin; know and believe that you are only one capricious decision away from being thrown out on the street. If you show that you're too people-oriented, someone may make that decision.

Rule 7: Do not display or condone aggressive behavior.

Organizations abhor aggressiveness. About the only time they don't hate it is when they are acting to get rid of someone who has displayed it. Then you'll see real aggression. As many careers have been shipwrecked on the shoals of aggressiveness as on any other hazard. Aggressiveness is one of those things that everyone says he or she values and believes he or she displays. It's sort of like honesty; most people lie like a rug (and I'm not criticizing the use of carefully planned lies at work) but feel guilty and say that they believe in telling the truth. We all lie all the time, and we wouldn't have it any other way. The same situation applies with aggressiveness. Everyone talks about how "we need a few aggressive people around here to breathe fire into this company."

While most people recognize that extreme aggressiveness would be job suicide, some will believe that lesser displays of aggressiveness are acceptable to the organization. They are not. Aggressiveness means change. After all, you can't "aggressively" maintain the routine. We owe our romantic preoccupation with aggressiveness to the orientation of our civilization and its emphasis on individual efforts to have an effect on the world. The only effect you'll get from being aggressive at work will be an opportunity for you to get intimately acquainted with the job market in your field long before you've got your résumé ready to go. Talk a lot about how aggressive you are, talk about how you value aggressiveness, and then demonstrate your aggressiveness by aggressively following this rule and not demonstrating any aggressiveness at all.

Rule 8: Do not threaten an organization's bureaucracies.

Even the leanest organization is sinfully overstaffed. And even the most personnel-burdened organization sees itself as lean and mean. This is because organizations are not composed of the one large bureaucracy that they appear to be. Each organization actually consists of many smaller groups. Each of these individual groups fervently establishes and maintains its own bureaucracy. Much more energy is spent in protecting and justifying these bureaucracies than is used to do the work of the organization. Just note how eagerly and gleefully one department will cheat another in order to obtain an additional job slot, even if the first department could use the slot more effectively for the organization's benefit. How often have you heard of a department head volunteering to cut back his or her own staff so that another department could better use the slots for the organization's benefit? On the very rare occasions when such a rational move is suggested by a sincere person who wants to get the work done more efficiently, it usually gets a reception similar to the following one.

Mary (a management trainee in Manufacturing): "Mr. Jones, have you seen the plan that Ms. Johnson developed? It'll cut overall personnel by 23 percent and decrease our back-order time by 8 percent! It looks like it can increase our bottom line by 11 percent in the first year, even after the capital expense."

Mr. Jones (VP of Manufacturing): "Yes, Mary, I saw it. Do you realize that over half of those eliminated slots will come out of our department? I don't know what they're trying to do with these crazy plans."

Mary: "But won't it help the company if we modernize and cut back on manual assembly?"

Mr. Jones: "Mary, you're young, and you're new here. You don't understand how these things operate. Manufacturing is the heart of this company. It always has been, and it always will be. We can handle our own problems without a lot of interference from outsiders like those meddlers in Finance."

Mary just came face to face with the strength of this perversion. Why is it so strong? It's very simple: It's difficult for people to identify strongly with a large group. Smaller groups tend to be more homogeneous than big ones. (You know what to expect and can fit in easier with a small group.) In fact, even groups of twenty or thirty are too big to maintain uniform roles and norms for their members. For this reason, you will usually find a lot of five-to-ten-person groups within a department, each of which has its own set of rules and perhaps even its own mini-bureaucracy. Any attack on what looks like one large bureaucracy is actually an attack on these powerful, fervently supported smaller groups. Do not waste your energy in attempts to overthrow or reduce bureaucracies. Concentrate instead on surviving within them.

Rule 9: Support the organization's inflated beliefs about its abilities, technologies, and strengths.

All organizations think they're better than they really are. After all, have you ever heard a company president say, "Well, we're not much of a company technically, but it's a comfortable place to work"? Of course not. Every organization believes that it's right at the top of the pile. You'd better behave as if you believe it, too. One of my best friends once worked as an executive for a baking company that made endless claims about the quality of its product. The company took great pains to brag about "real European bakers" in its media efforts (when, in fact, most of the plants across the country operated with low-paid workers who, at best, might have trained under a European baker for a few months). The presence of the imported bakers was that organization's rather weak claim to technical superiority in its field. The problem was that the European bakers, who were hired by and reported directly to the company president, were generally mediocre. My friend was continually battling with the corporate types who would chastise him for poor-quality products. Rather than just take the abuse, my friend repeatedly pointed out that the problems were caused by the inept bakers over whom he had little control. He did not realize that product quality was not an issue. In fact, the product that was produced in his plant was as good as and in many cases better than that produced by the other plants around the country. Product quality was not the real issue. Every division manager was continually blamed for product quality as part of the "quality is our emphasis" game. Eventually, the president fired him because "things just weren't working out." So, after tripling volume in ten months and increasing profits to 20 percent before taxes, he was out. And he deserved it. He didn't support the organization's beliefs in its superiority. The fact that such beliefs were false was totally irrelevant. The important job duties in that organization were to live with all the problems, flatter the president, talk a lot about quality but do nothing about it, focus only on volume, and just take the abuse when problems occurred. Don't let it happen to you. Support your organization's illusions of superiority in the face of reality, and your success won't be an illusion.

Rule 10: Always respect an organization's preference for seniority rather than performance.

We've all seen it—the employee who's been around forever and who doesn't do anything anymore. It's one thing to sit on your laurels, but for forty years? Well, don't even think about it. You're not the first one to notice, and you're not the only one who knows. The very presence of such senior employees is a comfort to all of those whose fears require that they believe the organization will care for them. Of course, the organization won't (Rule 3), but emotion, not reason, is relevant here. If you attempt to do anything other than display benign neglect toward these employees, you will suffer for it.

For example, Jane has just been hired from the outside by ABC Company to take over the Finance department. Along with an office, a dying diffenbachia, fourteen staffers, and an antiquated accounting system installed thirty years ago by her predecessor, Jane has also inherited Brad. Brad has been the assistant director of Finance for five years and has been with ABC Company for thirty-two years. Brad knows everyone in the company over fifty years old; belongs to every company group, team, and committee; and is on a first-name basis with every senior manager. Brad has never worked for another company. In his thirty-two years, Brad has been in fourteen different jobs in eight different departments. Despite outstanding ineptitude and total nonperformance, Brad survived. His survival is not an issue anymore; he's in for the duration. Jane's future, however, may not be that secure.

J.B.: "Well, Jane, how's your first week going?"
Jane: "Not so good, J.B. The financials are so disorganized, it's hard to tell where we stand."
J.B.: "Well, I'm sure you'll fix it. That's what we hired you for. By the way, how are you getting on with Brad?"

Jane: "Well, J.B., I'm glad you asked. There are some problems there. Brad doesn't seem to have any idea of what's going on. He can't explain where some of the numbers are coming from. On top of that, he spends all day talking on the phone with his friends or visiting around the company. I think we've got to consider getting him out of there."

J.B. (hikes himself up in his chair and stares straight at Jane): "Jane, you're new here. Brad has been with this company for thirty-two years. Why, I worked with him when my father brought me into the business after I graduated from Harvard. He taught me everything I know about sales during the first year I was here. I'm sure you'll find Brad an invaluable resource once you get your bearings."

A smart Jane would have answered J.B.'s original "How are things going?" question differently.

Smart Jane: "Great, J.B., just great! I can't tell you what a help it is to have Brad there to show me the ropes. The two of us are going to get things shaped up in short order."

J.B. would have loved Jane and passed along the compliment to Brad, who would then have said good things about Jane to all of his friends. Jane would have been in like a porch climber. She could have then ignored Brad's social activities and gotten on with her job. With fourteen other people, it wouldn't be hard to get along without Brad's efforts, especially since he had never done any work in the first place. Instead, Jane created a problem that will take months of careful rule following to fix.

The odds are that any employee like Brad who is there when you arrive will be there until he or she dies or retires. If cost cutting and personnel reductions are essential to your success, target younger and newer employees; like you, they are considered almost worthless to the organization. If such a senior employee actually does anything at all that is perceived as useful, he or she is even more untouchable and may play a role in policy making and the evaluation of new talent. If that's the case, treat the employee as you would an executive; avoid him or her as much as possible and flatter him or her vigorously when you can't.

Rule 11: Always treat executives as if they are special.

Executives think they are special. And the higher up they are, the more special they think they are. You'd better treat them like you believe it, too. Of course, executives are special; they make a lot of money. If they are earning their money by their contributions to the organization, they deserve proportionate rewards. Of course, no contributions can justify some of the excessive salaries they pay themselves, but salaries are beside the point. The salaries are merely one tangible aspect of the respect to which they feel they're entitled. They want much more than money from you. They expect respect for their knowledge and wisdom, deference to their every wish, obeisance, and credit for everything good that happens. If something bad happens, it's the economy, government regulations, unfair competition, or your fault. Most of them even want and expect all of the employees actually to like them. It's a sad situation but one that's not apt to change. It won't make it any easier to live with, but I'll explain why executives think this way.

Most executives are surrounded either by expert rule followers or world-class yes-men. In such company, they seldom hear any criticism, arguments, or challenges to their decisions. An occasional misguided employee (one who's actually trying to get the job done) sneaks through the protective cordon with the truth every once in a while, but such rare events only reinforce the executives' beliefs. The deviant is seen as a troublemaker, and his or her career is gleefully snuffed out by the executive entourage. Everything in the executive world reinforces their belief that they are special. The furniture is nice, and the secretaries are always available to fetch coffee, get the paper, run around town to do errands, balance their personal checkbooks, dial the phone, and screen out undesirables who want them to make decisions. On top of that, there are special parking spots, special cafeterias, first-class air travel, the best restaurants and hotels, interest-free loans, company-paid cars, and golden parachute contracts so they'll be rich for life if they get thrown out for ruining the company. And then they get paid from $50,000 to $200,000 or more per year. It's rough at the top!

People in general quickly and readily adapt their self-concepts to their perceptions of their environment. When surrounded with the accoutrements of wealth and power, it's often easier for executives to come to the belief that they're special, that they alone caused it, and that they deserve it, rather than to realize that many successes are incredible artifacts of the way things worked out (not to mention the efforts of the employees). Executives are very good at assuming that they have done it all themselves (even if they did it by being the children of the owner). You'll go further if you help them maintain this erroneous self-perception.

Rule 12: Stay away from executives at all times.

Everyone has this fantasy once in a while. You're working late on some meaningless piece of busy work, and the chairman of the board walks into your office. He just flew in to check up on the division's poor performance. It's a holiday evening, and you're the only one in the whole fifty-story building. The lonely chairman asks you out to dinner at a posh restaurant. Over dinner, you tell him how it really is back at the office. You present a few of your plans. When the reorganization comes in a week or so, you're named as the new president of the division, with the chairman's ear and carte blanche to get things moving. The truth is that no executive (except your boss if he or she is one of them) is going to be able to do anything of substance to help your career. However, one small wrong move with an executive can cause all sorts of career problems. Unnecessary contact with executives is far too dangerous to risk for the rare and minor tangible good that it might do your career. The remaining rules in this chapter will detail the proper attitude and demeanor toward executives. (This means the brass to whom you don't report. The rules for boss management are presented in Chapter 6.) However, no matter what the situation, you'll minimize potential career damage by minimizing your contact with executives as much as possible.

Rule 13: Do not blindly trust the judgment or intelligence of executives and senior management.

Do not make the mistake of equating office square footage and salary size with competence and wisdom. While you must act as if you believe there is a direct relationship (Rule 11), do not take information and ideas from these people at face value. If you are in a situation where your fate rests on a program decision, do not believe that some executive or senior management type knows more about it than you do. Such people are no more naturally gifted than similarly educated and mature adults like yourself. If you are not forced by circumstances to do it their way, give your own ideas and those of your colleagues at least equal consideration. The executive who cavalierly tosses out flip solutions to your problems won't be the one to suffer if you try it his or her way and things don't work out.

Just as important to your long-term success is your understanding that executives do not get to the top because they are better than you are. If you get depressed and confused when you see obviously limited individuals in such positions, you'll lose your stomach for the long struggle ahead. When you see some obviously mediocre executive, it's easy to wonder if there is some hidden or magic gift, skill, or intelligence that these people have but you can't even recognize. There is no mystery. People who have worked their way up to the top are either great natural rule followers or were incredibly lucky. Don't let the apparent mystical success of obviously limited people lead you into depression, desperation, or surrender.

Rule 14: Do not try to tell executives about problems.

Executives get paid to make policy and planning decisions. Other people get paid to manage the day-to-day operations of the organization. That's the way it's supposed to work. Even if the executives knew or understood the elements of day-to-day operations (and they usually don't), they should be working so hard at long-range planning and strategy that they don't have time to get involved with their subordinates' responsibilities. Executives do not know or care about what is going on in the bowels of the organization. Naive employees often think that executives would be grateful if they really knew what was going on. This mistaken and dangerous notion results from the limited perspective that these budding career failures possess.

The naive employee sees problems and transgressions as serious drains on overall efficiency (which they are, of course, but don't forget that performance is a minor consideration). They assume that the top brass would be interested in hearing about it. Forget it. The brass have the same types of problems with the people at their own level. If they can't fix it at their level, they sure don't want to hear about it at yours. Even more hazardous to your career is the fact that the executives themselves may be committing or causing the same types of problems that you're reporting (which explains why it is instant career death to complain to an executive about incompetence).

Sometimes it will seem as if an executive is sincerely and eagerly interested in hearing the truth. Don't believe it. Executives always ask about problems as part of the ritual of showing their "concern." For example, J.B. is walking through the building on his way to the maintenance shop in order to find out why the maintenance crew hasn't completed the refinishing of his four coffee tables and ten dining room chairs. He meets Mary, the manager of Data Input, in the hallway. Mary is on her way to the maintenance shop to find out why the air conditioning in her department hasn't been fixed since she put in the job order two weeks ago.

J.B.: "Well, Mary, how are things going?"

Mary: "Just fine, sir. Everything is fine."

J.B.: "No problems? Nothing I can help with?"

Here, J.B. is playing the ritual a little more aggressively because he'll feel even better if he digs for problems and doesn't find any. He can convince himself that he's really got things running well.

Mary: "No, sir. Absolutely not, sir. Everything is fine. Incidentally, I'd like to compliment you on the fine speech you gave at the retirement and awards dinner last week. Everybody was talking about it. Well, I've got to get to a meeting. It was nice to talk with you. I'll see you later, sir."

This was a fine performance. Mary didn't rise to the false bait and tell J.B. about her problems, she flattered him a little, and then she got out of there fast. J.B. will have a fine feeling toward Mary that will color all of his future decisions concerning her career. Note what happens if Mary isn't a good rule follower.

Mary: "Well, to tell you the truth, J.B., I'm having a lot of trouble getting the air conditioning in my department fixed. The temperature is over 97 degrees, and a lot of the older people are getting sick. The manager of the maintenance shop told me he has a big furniture-refinishing job to take care of before he can fix the air conditioner. Could you see what you can do? We've got fans going, but it's just too hot. Twenty percent of my people had to leave early today alone!"

J.B. (speaking): Well, Mary, I'll look into it. I'm sure they're doing their best on it. They're very busy on a lot of important projects."

(thinking): "What's with her? Here I am, the president and owner of ABC Company, actually wasting my time talking to her, and she has the nerve to think her air conditioning is more critical than my furniture? I'll tell Jack to stuff her job order in the trash."

Mary presented J.B. with a problem that she felt was critical to the company's efficiency. Unfortunately for Mary, J.B. has additional information and interests, the least of which is a few sick workers down on the tenth floor in Mary's department. If he doesn't get that furniture back soon, he's in big trouble at home. It's the same in all organizations.

Rather than deal with the very real problems that you might bring to their attention, executives will view you as a troublemaker, a rule breaker, and not very good management material. Keep it to yourself.

Rule 15: Do not be surprised when the words and actions of executives don't match.

Observe how John, the Compensation and Benefits manager, deals with an instance of the "executive word and executive actions" paradox.

John: "J.B., you said last week at the retirement dinner that ABC Company was going to do everything it could to make this a fun place to work. In keeping with that philosophy, I've taken the liberty of drawing up a plan for a day-care center. Based on a review of our demographics and a preliminary cost study, it looks like it would just about support itself. The benefit to our recruiting program and the reduction of strain on our employees would be tremendous."

J.B.: "Yes, yes, I see *(meaning that he doesn't)*. That's a very interesting idea *(meaning that he thinks it's absurd)*. Imagine, a day-care center for children right here at ABC Company *(meaning that he can't imagine it at all)*. Why don't you just leave it here, and I'll take a look at it when I have the time *(meaning that if he has time, he'll glance at it as it falls from his hand into the trash can)*."

(Two months later)

John: "Hello, J.B. Say, have you had a chance to look at my proposal for the day-care center?"

J.B.: "Oh, yes, John. I reviewed it in detail *(meaning that he tossed it out the day John gave it to him)*. After much thought *(about a nanosecond)* I've come to the conclusion that it's just not something that would fit here at ABC Company."

A smart, rule-following John: "You know best, J.B. Thanks for taking the time to review it."

A not-so-smart John: "I don't understand, J.B. You said at the retirement dinner that...."

The sordid details of not-so-smart John's career progression from that point on are too unpleasant to relate here. Do not frustrate yourself and waste energy by attempting to reconcile the irreconcilable.

Rule 16: Do not expect executives to deal with you honestly and candidly.

Executives mistrust the sincerity and intentions of their subordinates. Wouldn't you? If you were the typical executive, you'd be overpaid and overpampered. A lot of people would want your job. Nobody would dare argue with you for fear of losing their jobs or their status. Few people would ever say what they really mean because you would have surrounded yourself with expert rule followers and yes-men. It is a good point to make the distinction between rule followers and yes-men. Those who follow the rules employ flattery as just one of many tools in their arsenal of coldly and objectively applied business success maneuvers. Simple yes-men have but one tool, and they apply it emotionally in every situation regardless of its applicability. In any case, the typical executive receives a lot of compliments and strokes. Given that mind set, you can understand why even the most straightforward procedural suggestion may be incorrectly interpreted as a power move by the listening executive. For example, Gregg, the VP of Marketing, has come up with a plan to reorganize the marketing and client services area. He thinks the new arrangement will eliminate a nagging problem.

> *Gregg:* "Say, J.B., I think I've got something here that will take care of all the conflicts between reorders and production scheduling for new customers. I think I've addressed everything from the order input system to follow-through on customer service."
>
> *J.B. (speaking):* "Good, good. Let me take a look at that here. That's just what we've been looking for."
>
> *(thinking):* "Great. Just what I need. One more long-winded report that I didn't ask for. I should have been a doctor; I'd be playing golf now."
>
> *Gregg:* "As you can see, we'll be able to process all orders faster and still have the capability to handle another 25 percent without additional personnel when the Jenkins deal comes through."
>
> *J.B. (speaking):* "Very impressive. This is a very comprehensive plan."
>
> *(thinking):* "Sigh. And I suppose you'll want more people, more money, a bigger office, a desk like mine, and half of the customer service staff to report to you."
>
> *Gregg:* "Of course, if we do it, it means the customer service area, particularly in systems, is going to have to coordinate their production

scheduling with sales. There's going to have to be a central point for decisions on priorities.''

> *J.B. (speaking)*: ''Well, that's really just a minor detail. I'm sure we can work something out.''
>
> *(thinking)*: ''I knew it! This guy thinks he can slick J.B.? I knew this was a power play from the minute I heard the words 'got something here.' I hope he doesn't hold his breath on getting this one by me. Now I know why the manager of Customer Service was in here yesterday whining about trouble between the departments.''

J.B. expected a power play, and he was going to find one if he had to dig a ditch to find it. Executives react like this because they've been doing the same things themselves for years. They're sensitive to all the signs they try so hard to hide when they're making a power play of their own.

4

Rules for General Demeanor at Work

It makes no sense to go to all the trouble of doing such things as managing yourself, your boss, and your employees according to the rules if you're going to turn around and ruin all of the effort by lapses in more basic areas. Since these more basic "general demeanor" areas seem so mundane, they are often overlooked. Ambitious go-getters just like yourself will spare no effort in getting in good with the boss and spouting all the latest MBA jargon but will neglect equally important factors that don't appear as critical. This is a big mistake. Lapses in proper personal appearance, courtesy, and overall demeanor can be just as deadly as arguing with the boss or complaining about the bureaucracy to the president's secretary. Every day you have hundreds of interactions with other employees in which general demeanor factors are being evaluated. Every second you're in the plant or office, every minute people can see you, any time you're talked to or about, general demeanor factors are being evaluated. You've got to be on stage with the proper general demeanor every second.

Rule 17: Demonstrate exceptional courtesy and respect for every person in every situation.

Although nobody likes to admit it, we have a caste system in this country. It's based upon perceived power and wealth. Higher-caste members automatically assume that the lower-caste members are less intelligent, less sensitive, and less worthy of respect. Caste distinctions are made mostly on the basis of visual cues such as clothing, cars, and social position (whom you are seen with). Don't try to tell yourself that you don't make the same distinctions. When was the last time you said "Thank you, ma'am" to the cleaning lady? When was the last time you answered a question from the elderly maintenance man with a crisp "Yes, sir"? If you allow yourself to slip into this caste mentality, you'll begin automatically to assign people to a caste on very scanty information. If you allow this quite natural tendency to take over, you'll not only leave yourself open to the possibility of making some serious mistakes but you'll also lose many valuable opportunities to enhance your general image.

I once worked with an arrogant young man who got himself into a career-damaging situation because of a caste identification error. The fellow was a young hot-shot MBA who was on the way up. He always spouted the very latest MBA jargon, wore the best suits, acted like a total snob to everybody beneath him on the organization chart, and drove the newest red Porsche, which he always managed to park right next to "Executive Row" in the parking lot (so that they could see that he was there early). One manifestation of his all-encompassing arrogance was this person's incredibly rude driving behavior. One morning as he approached the freeway off-ramp near the office, he got stuck behind an old, beat-up Cadillac that was burning oil like a tramp steamer as it inched up the ramp. Anxious lest he should lose out on the first parking space next to Executive Row, he hit the horn and swerved from side to side, looking for an opportunity to pass on the ramp shoulder. Such an opportunity didn't present itself, and he was forced to follow along in the smokescreen until the two cars arrived at the stoplight at the bottom of the ramp. In a rage, he pulled up next to the old Cadillac, hit the horn, stuck out his middle finger, and remained in that pose until the light changed and he screeched off. As he walked from his car into the building, guess what car drove into the president's spot? The president's Mercedes was in the shop for work, and his secretary (who gleefully recounted the events of the morning to any and all) was using her son's car to give him a lift. Although the president said and did nothing that day, Mr. Arrogance was no longer creating havoc with traffic patterns in the area of that particular organization two months later. It is doubtful that he would have been so discourteous to the driver of an expensive new car. His automatic assignment of people to castes and his differential treatment of them caused him great distress. Small caste assignment errors can do a lot of damage.

Even more important than decreasing the odds of making an identity error on a VIP is the habit strength you'll build up by being courteous to everyone. When you get tense and possibly angry, you'll respond by habit. You want these habits to result in behaviors that will enhance your low, positive profile, not to create problems. All people have the same needs for respect and esteem. If you give them courtesy, they will, for the most part, return it. Whenever anyone helps you in any way, no matter how minor, always answer, "Thank you, sir/ma'am." When someone asks you a question that requires a yes or no answer, always answer, "Yes/no, sir/ma'am," no matter what the age or status of the questioner. (If your organization is particularly cutthroat, you might have to consciously avoid using such courtesy with peers; it may give the impression that you're weak or timid or that you feel others are better than you are.) You'll be amazed at the way they'll love it. Continual and constant courtesy will make your day-to-day work easier. Remember, the low-caste members are the ones who do most of your dirty work. If you treat them with dignity and respect, they'll not only work harder for you, but they'll also spread around a lot of good press because they probably won't get such consideration from many other people.

An additional strategy that you can use to enhance your general reputation is to get into the habit of thanking people you work with for their valuable contributions at every opportunity. Even if they didn't do anything of substance, thank them. Tell them, "I look forward to working with you again." Tell them, "I really appreciate the time you've spent with me on this effort." Tell them, "It's nice to work with someone who takes real pride in their work." Tell them whatever you think you can get away with. This will leave them with the impression that you like them and are grateful for what they did.

Rule 18: Keep a tight rein on your emotions at all times.

This is one of the most important rules. It is also one of the most difficult to follow. We are creatures of emotion more than we are rational thinkers. From second to second, we react emotionally to almost everything in our environment, from what people say to how they look to what we think about things others do. Everyone has emotional reactions all the time. Yet almost any display of emotion is inappropriate at work. Even an outburst of enthusiasm and happiness at landing a multi-million-dollar deal could be detrimental to your career. You would be viewed as being immature and not professional. (Being "professional" is a big thing in business. It generally means acting distant, calm, and unemotional at all times.) When you are in your first few junior positions, displays of enthusiasm and happiness over company triumphs are tolerated as natural exuberance. Executives will condescendingly tolerate a degree of this in junior personnel because it allows them to reflect on the days when they were young, enthusiastic, and "in the trenches." Once you have left the junior ranks, such displays of enthusiasm are serious mistakes. Even more damning are displays of temper. One outburst, whatever the reason, could forever ruin your chances in an organization. Peoples' fear of losing control of themselves is probably at the bottom of this almost pathological obsession against even reasonable displays of emotion. When someone loses his or her temper or rolls on the floor with laughter, all those who see it are reminded of their own potential for emotional behavior. This reaction is even more extreme when the observers have low self-images; they are threatened by persons who are self-assured enough not to worry about what others think. The display of such emotional behavior would be indicative not so much of self-assurance as of someone who is not smart enough to know the rule. Emotions have a place, but it is not at work.

Rule 19: Never display a sense of humor.

Humor is like aggressiveness and honesty; everyone likes to think that they demonstrate it, hardly anybody does, and, if they could, they probably wouldn't. A good sense of humor requires that the user demonstrate a certain amount of playfulness and childlike qualities during the expression of the humor. In the terminology of transactional analysis, the archetype (child) aspect of the ego comes into play. This is viewed as a display of emotion and is thus a violation of Rule 18 in and of itself. Of course, many humorous situations and comments can be precipitated without displays of emotion. Humor is dangerous for a more important reason. It is rare that a joke or comment does not demean some group or characteristic. Even the most obtuse, innocent humor can cause problems.

Consider what happened to a friend of mine and one of his colleagues. My friend was always forced to arrive at work at around 6:45 A.M. in order to avoid two hours of bumper-to-bumper, nerve-shattering traffic.

His senior colleague lived only five miles from the office but could not deal with the bumper-to-bumper, nerve-shattering guilt of allowing anyone else to get to the office sooner than he did. So nobody ever got to the office earlier than the two of them. On his first day of a two-week-long visit, the West Coast company president came in at 7:45 A.M. and was visibly disappointed when he saw the coffee made and the two workers sitting in one of the offices talking (with a lot of papers spread around to make it appear as if they were working; see Rule 26). The president said something like, "You fellows sure get here early." They agreed and mentioned their work load. Each day, the president arrived fifteen minutes earlier than the previous day, but to no avail. The coffee was always made and half used (as they did, it's a good idea to pour half of it out when you work this ploy; it makes it seem as if you've been there two or three cups "longer"). By the fourth day, the president realized he was beaten. Since he couldn't win, he decided to "join the group" in the group dynamics sense. That is, since he couldn't win the battle, he wanted even more to be a member of the "early arrivers" in order to reduce his guilt and allow himself to maintain his self-image as someone who works so hard he's in the "always at the office first" group.

This is a common ploy on the part of persons who can't measure up on a dimension that they feel is critical. Rather than attempt to achieve on the dimension in question, they seek affiliation with a group that possesses the dimension. In order to join the early arrivers group, the president began to get more informal and friendly. They, in turn, violated Rule 25 and became more informal with him (rather than pretending to be more informal while carefully remaining cold and calculating). One morning, in the midst of their humorous bantering about the effects of long work hours, my friend performed his famous imitation of a hunchback while contending that long hours had no effect on him. His colleague threw in a few quick ones about Quasimodo and bells. Everyone laughed. They figured they had made points. They found out what kind of points the next Monday at lunchtime when the president's wife was introduced to everyone. You guessed it: She had a hump in the middle of her back. They earned points all right. They had violated a cardinal rule and gambled on the odds. They lost.

Rule 20: Never use sarcasm, irony, or puns at work.

This rule is presented as separate from Rule 19 for a very practical reason. Most of you probably don't view sarcastic remarks, puns, and ironic comments as outright humor. Many bright people view the use of sarcasm and irony as an almost sacred right. It allows them to display their cynicism, keen intellects, and fast minds. They are generally intelligent but somewhat bitter and frustrated people who consider the use of sarcasm and wit as their sacred right in payment for all of the frustrations they suffer at the hands of the organization. They are making a big mistake. First of all, excessive use of sarcasm and puns quickly comes to be viewed by others as emotionally based and thus not "professional." You don't have to be a psychologist to recognize this type of motivation when you see it. Insecure people view any sarcastic remarks as direct attacks on themselves or the organization. This will occur even if the motivation for the remark is purely recreational. It's the implied disrespect for the organization that causes the negative reaction in other people. They are extremely sensitive to very small amounts of it.

Even in small doses, sarcasm, irony, and puns are dangerous. The basis for this additional danger is twofold. First of all, many people have no sense of humor at all and will interpret all remarks absolutely literally. As an example of how a little sarcasm can cause a big problem when it passes unnoticed as sarcasm, consider the following situation. Sally, the VP of Manufacturing, reads a terrible report from Lloyd in Finance about the potential of the Jenkins deal. As usual, Lloyd has demonstrated his complete lack of knowledge of finance, marketing, and operations. Shortly thereafter, Sally is meeting with the president about another project.

J.B.: "Incidentally, Sally, what did you think of Lloyd's analysis of the Jenkins deal?"

Sally (wanting to shaft Lloyd and demonstrate her wit): "Oh, it was really great!" *(with sarcasm dripping from her words like water off a bird dog).*

J.B. (completely deadpan): "Well, I wasn't very impressed. I'm surprised that you didn't see the obvious problems with it."

Now what does she do? Does she tell J.B. that she was only being sarcastic and that he didn't catch it, or does she just let him go on thinking that she's as much of an idiot as Lloyd? Sally has been hoist by her own sarcastic petard. She will have to twist in the wind for many weeks (or months) while she attempts to repair the damage with scrupulously careful rule following.

The second danger that arises from the use of sarcasm, irony, and puns evolves from the sorry fact that a lot of people are too intellectually limited to be able to understand the intent of sarcastic remarks, particularly if they contain even the most elementary literary and theatrical references. The danger is that those who don't understand the pun will dimly realize that they're too slow to catch on and will be offended that you are "playing with them," even if you aren't. Note the effect when Patrick the punster tries to be cute while Mort and Debbie are talking at the coffee machine.

Mort: "Well, Debbie, how did it go at the convention?"

Debbie: "Great, Mort, just great. I got a chance to sit on a committee with the famous Mr. Kent, who designed the B-78 widget!"

Patrick: "Isn't he the guy who had to wear the same suit for three years because he lost his telephone credit card?" *(a rather obvious reference to Clark Kent's use of phonebooths as dressing rooms).*

Debbie (understanding the pun and running with it): "Yeah, but he could really make a long distance call when he got those leotards off!"

Mort (speaking): "Huh?"

(thinking): "What are they talking about?"

Patrick: "Was he really a man of steel?"

Debbie: "Yeah, but I let him have it with my Debbienite. That turned him into the al dente man!"

At this point, Debbie and Patrick are totally out of control and will keep punning on the Superman theme until they use it up. Meanwhile, Mort has been totally humiliated by his inability to either understand or contribute. If his temperament is so inclined, he may later get even by mentioning to someone that Patrick and Debbie were wasting a lot of time by the coffee machine. Save yourself a lot of trouble and stay away from irony, sarcasm, and puns. Control your bitterness and channel it into careful rule following rather than sarcasm; you'll go farther.

Rule 21: Avoid dirty tricks and power plays at all times.

Every few years there is a spate of books and articles about the strategy and tactics of using dirty tricks in the office and how to advance your career by intentionally hurting others. As detailed in Chapter 2, our attachment with these types of techniques is romantic; the crafty, cool-mannered manipulator appeals to the Machiavellian in all of us. One such book outlines detailed procedures for, among other pleasantries, ruining a rival's briefing by making noises, arriving late, and squeaking your chair on the floor. The book also describes tactics for convincing rivals that someone else is out to get them so that they will start a conflict that will ruin them both and leave the door open for you. Forget it; these techniques require steel nerves, less than gifted targets, a natural ability that few of us possess, and luck, which you have no rational reason to expect. Dirty tricks require careful planning and a lot of energy. If you aren't already obeying all of the rules perfectly, you can't afford to waste your time and energy by deliberately trying to hurt your rivals; you're already hurting yourself by not taking care of the more important basics first. Even more damning is the revenge factor. If there's anything that gets limited people more upset than being eclipsed by someone smarter than they are, it's having someone smarter than they are try to make them look even worse on purpose. If your attempts are exposed, you will be open to all sorts of backroom slander and personality assassination.

If you get reckless and lock horns with someone who's intelligent and perceptive, both of your careers will be consumed in the conflagration. Open corporate warfare between gifted rivals generates a lot of attention, all of it bad. By the time it's over, it won't matter who won the battle; both parties' careers will have lost the war. If the conflicts become really nasty and attract a lot of attention, the brass is going to start wondering if maybe the organization's reputation, not to mention the quality of its work, is suffering through neglect. Stay away from dirty tricks; they're just not worth it.

Rule 22: Avoid sexual liaisons at the office at all costs.

The kiss you get at the office could well be the kiss of death to your job. Every large and most small organizations are rife with stories about sexual liaisons between members. While there inevitably is more talk than action, scores of people are compromising their careers by engaging in sexual liaisons at the office. Avoid them at all costs. They can never help, and they always cause damage. Others will find out. And when they do you will no longer be Mr. or Ms. Business; you will merely be an object of sexual interest. More attention will be focused on derogatory discussions of your physical assets than on your work. Those persons who possess a bent for hypocritical moralizing will have a field day.

For example, consider the following exchange between Nancy, a department supervisor, and Ms. Jacobs, the VP of Manufacturing, as they sit in the company cafeteria during lunch. They see Derek, a corporate officer, walk through the line, get lunch, and join an attractive young lady at a corner table. At this point, Nancy and Ms. Jacobs are unaware that Derek and the young lady have been having an affair.

Nancy: "Oh, there's Derek Smith. Isn't he handsome?"

Ms. Jacobs: "Yes, he's quite an attractive man. He's made some great deals for the company over the past few years. From what I understand, he's working on a merger now that will give us the edge in high-tech widgets."

Nancy: "Yes, I heard him speak at the Monday morning briefing last week, and he talked about it a little. He's really a good speaker. And so handsome!"

No problem so far. Both women respect Derek for his work. Nancy will have to learn to watch her emotional behavior with an executive, but it's not a problem in this situation. Although neither would admit it (which is smart), both of them are wondering what it would be like to be involved romantically with Derek. It's a natural and healthy passing fantasy that they both enjoy as they eat lunch and talk. Now, notice the change in Nancy's perception of Derek three days later. She's having lunch with Bob, a secretary in her department. Since her lunch with Ms. Jacobs, Nancy has heard through the grapevine about Derek's affair with his lunchtime companion.

Nancy (smirking): "There's that stud Smith with that slut. I wonder if they've done it yet today?"

Bob: "No wonder he always looks so refreshed. I wonder if they do it on that leather couch in his office?"

Nancy is letting her jealousy show through, but it's Derek who has the problem. He's lost the respect of most of the organization, and that will hurt him in a thousand little ways. Derek will no longer bask in the unsolicited good press that everybody used to pass around because they admired him and enjoyed making him appear bigger than life. Instead, Derek's career will be buffeted by a lot of negative stuff that everyone will gleefully generate and embellish for a few laughs. Of course, Nancy will have to learn to watch how she talks to junior-level staffers, but that's a small problem compared to the one that Derek has created for himself.

Women are even more at risk than men. The strong remnants of our double-standard sexual mores and the jealousy of other men will lead people to condemn a woman for a perfectly reasonable sexual liaison that might not have been worthy of note if a man was the subject of discussion. And if the affair is less than ecstatic, and problems arise and get publicized, you are in deep trouble.

Rule 23: Never complain to anyone about anything.

Sooner or later it will get back to the people involved in the worst possible way. Look what happens to poor Fred.

Fred (having just had his car smashed in the parking lot by the trash truck, complains to his secretary): "I can't believe this place! Whoever laid out that parking lot design was an idiot. The garbage truck didn't have enough room, and the idiot driver smashed my car!"

This complaint is overheard by Lloyd, one of Fred's rivals, who also reports to J.B. Lloyd happens to know that J.B. is an avid amateur parking lot designer and was responsible for the parking lot design. The next time Lloyd is in J.B.'s office, he puts the overheard remark to use.

Lloyd: "Well, I hate to be the one to tell you, J.B., but Fred thinks you're an idiot. He told everyone within earshot the other day. I'm only telling you this because I'm worried about the effect that sort of thing has on morale."

The only morale that Lloyd was concerned with was his own if he didn't get a chance to tell J.B. about Fred's remark. Of course, Fred doesn't have the slightest idea who laid out the parking lot; he couldn't care less. He was just letting off steam. But he complained about someone and left himself open.

It's a strange thing, but all but the most morally degenerate people have difficulties telling complete falsehoods, but they will work like dedicated master craftsmen in order to embroider and embellish half truths. One reason for this is that they realize that it's much harder for you to defend yourself against a half truth than it is to defend yourself against a raging, gaping lie. Consider the plight of John, a management trainee at ABC Company. In a conversation with Lloyd, John had said, "You know, that Ms. Jacobs does one great job in running production. She's a real hard-ass when it comes to dealing with quality problems." To you and me, that sounds like the compliment it was meant to be. To Lloyd, a master at the art of half-truth embellishment, it is an opportunity to hurt John and cause a little trouble in general. Lloyd proceeds to spread around the "news" that "John said that Ms. Jacobs is a hard-ass.'' A week later, John is in a meeting with Ms. Jacobs.

Ms. Jacobs: ''John, it's come to my attention that you have been telling people that I'm a hard-ass. Is that true?''

What can John say that won't make it worse? It will be hard to explain that he said it but that it was meant as a compliment and that he only said it to Lloyd. She already thinks he's guilty and expects him to deny it. He might try the truth.

John: ''Well, Ms. Jacobs, I did say you were a hard-ass about quality, but I meant it as a compliment.''

Ms. Jacobs will most likely consider it a total admission of guilt. If she believes him, she'll assume he isn't too discreet. In any case, she'll associate him with a negative event. Or he could deny it.

John: ''No, ma'am, I did not. Whoever told you that is lying.''

He's actually got a better chance here. But it's a bad scene for John's career any way he handles it.

A lot of people would never openly make a serious complaint about anything but don't pause for a second to whine and act impatient with ''the company way.'' Don't kid yourself; these little displays of impatience (''It takes forever to get expense reports paid around here!'') are just as dangerous to your career as more open and vicious complaints. Most organization members identify very strongly with the organization itself. Limited individuals do so even more strongly. Any sign of impatience with the way things are done, from clucking over how slow the cafeteria line is moving to discussing how long it takes to get approvals for projects, will be seen by these individuals as attacks on the company.

Rule 24: Do not attempt to impress anyone with your knowledge and experience.

You are at work only to succeed in your career and get the work done (in that order). If you get your work done, it will impress your boss. If you follow the rules, everything else will take care of itself. There is nothing to be gained by trying to impress the whole organization with your knowledge. There is much to lose. Rules 19 and 20 discussed the disadvantages of humor and wit. Hard Fact 10 (Chapter 3) did the same for general intelligence and creativity. The same disadvantages pertain to displays of expertise that involve your direct job responsibilities. Nobody likes a show-off, particularly if the show-off calls attention to their deficits. Your ego may get a short boost, but there will be no long-term boost. Observe the effect that Lloyd has on Mary when he puts her down during a meeting with J.B.

J.B.: "This report is very impressive, Mary. Yes, very impressive. Have you calculated the ROI in current dollars for the out years?"

Mary: "No, sir. I'm not sure how to do that without making some very subjective assumptions about the cost of raw materials.

Lloyd: "Oh, I can do that, J.B. It's really a very elementary technique that's taught in all the top schools. I learned the technique my first year at Sloan. I guess I shouldn't be too surprised that Mary here doesn't know about it."

Now Mary hates Lloyd and will not miss an opportunity to help him make a mistake if she can do so without getting caught. On the more positive side, Lloyd may have hurt himself because he will now have to produce, and he won't be able to distribute the responsibility as easily to Mary. If Lloyd was a follower of the rules, he would have responded to Mary's plight in the following way.

Lloyd: "J.B., I'd be glad to try and help Mary on that. I know a little something about a technique that may work. It'd be a shame not to take this excellent job the last few steps."

This response would have gotten Mary solidly on Lloyd's side, would have impressed J.B. as a good "team player" move, and (irrelevant as it may be to your career advancement and the orientation of this book) might have contributed toward getting the job done more effectively. But Lloyd will never learn. Count on it; bragging about or openly displaying your technical skills after you've been hired will alienate all of the less-skilled employees in your organization. You can't afford to have that many people upset with you.

Rule 25: Resist with all your strength the temptation to become more informal and relaxed with people at work as you get to know them.

Remember when you first started your most recent job? You were very careful about what you said, how you acted, and what you disclosed to your colleagues. As you began to think that everybody was "just plain folks," you began to loosen up. All of a sudden, you're telling raunchy jokes to the secretary you originally thought was so prim and proper and you're telling Mr. Company Man that you're not happy with the way things are being run. Most people do this, but, then again, most people aren't too bright. The people at work are not your friends. They are parts of an organization that will use you according to its own selfish needs, which change from one day to the next. Do not be fooled into thinking that your disclosures will not influence how you are evaluated.

It's easy to lose your perspective about getting close to people at work. The problem is that if you let yourself get closer to them and more comfortable with them, you'll start to react emotionally when you're around them. This will set you up for potentially damaging disclosures.

Even more incredible is the fact that many people deliberately disclose damaging information. For example, if they're looking for another job, or just want everyone to think they are, they'll put the word out on the grapevine by leaving a résumé in the copy machine or simply telling someone. They think they are punishing management by showing them that somebody doesn't like them. But management is not really worried about how you feel. However, they care a great deal about loyalty (Rule 3) and will punish those who do not display it. They could care less how you feel about the way things are going. Grow up and live with your problems. Do something to change your situation for the better. Blabbing to your fellow workers will not help.

Rule 26: Always appear to be busy and hard at work.

It is a sad fact that even in these times of economic turmoil and greater emphasis on productivity there are many jobs that don't provide enough work to keep an average person busy all day. This is particularly true of supervisory and management jobs. The problem is that the work levels of most of these jobs have been adjusted over time so that any minimally qualified person has a 90 percent chance of meeting the performance standards. You'll probably always have a lot of spare time on your hands. Don't assume that everyone will know that you are caught up with your work and will thus excuse what might appear to be loafing around. They will not make such assumptions. Remember that there are always some who are so limited that they are strained to the limits of their endurance just to handle coffee breaks. They will naturally assume that you are no smarter than they are and will think you are loafing around while they are killing themselves. ("Why, I only took a two-hour lunch and five breaks, only got here thirty minutes late, and look at Jones! He was sitting at his desk with his feet up! I wish I had the time to do that!") Anyone who sees it will view any newspaper reading, coffee breaks, chatting in the hallways, or personal phone calls as loafing regardless of your contributions. Managers who spend most of their time in the idle nonsense of off-site meetings, executive briefings, and just plain visiting, are even more hypocritical. Their view is that you should always be doing more for the company. That's nice in theory, but you often will have no outlet for more work. If you do more than the job offers, you'll end up getting in trouble for "stepping on other peoples' toes" (it wakes them up), "exceeding your authority" (it points up all the things they're not doing with their authority), and so on. Nevertheless, you must look busy at all times. Attempt to find useful, nonthreatening things to do. If worse comes to worse, write a few letters.

A former colleague of mine was hired by a large defense contractor as the manager of Executive Development. After taking the well-paying position and settling into her plush corner-window office, she discovered that there was no real work to do. The executives felt they were "developed" enough, and the organization wanted absolutely no changes in anything. How would you handle that situation? I hope you'd do just what my colleague did. She took a lot of seminars, traveled around the company to meet all the executives in order to get their first-hand input, wrote a lot of professional papers, and did a little organizational research on the rank and file (executives always think those beneath them need a lot of development). She looked busy, everyone liked her because she didn't push, she was visible and solicitous of their opinions, and she didn't make waves by pointing out all the real problems nobody wanted to acknowledge. At the same time, she built up her reputation within the management development community. Two years after taking the job, she was offered a more prestigious job for higher pay in a better-known company. She got the offer because one of the executives she met in the first job recommended her when he moved on. As it turned out, the new job was about the same as the first; lots of appearance but no opportunity to do significant things that could really help the bottom line. So now my former colleague is making $20,000 per year more than before and continuing to build her reputation while she looks for a real challenge. She hasn't found it yet, but nobody can say she's wasting her time. Look busy by working on things for yourself if there's nothing else to do and you can't lose.

Rule 27: Emulate as many of the habits of the upper management as you can.

Charles Caleb Colton wrote that imitation is the sincerest flattery. He might have gone far in today's business world. As an earlier rule (11) indicated, executives think they are special. They like to feel that they set the standards for proper, professional business behavior in their organization. If they're hot for a certain charity, the push is on for everybody to chip in big. If the chief executive likes to eat lunch at his or her desk, you may find that an expense report for a big restaurant lunch may run into trouble in Finance. It is essential to indicate by imitation that you respect the executives so much that you want to be just like they are. There are many obvious and easy ways to demonstrate this.

You can get a lot of mileage out of little things. Clothing styles are easy to emulate. If they wear three-piece suits, leave your Western stitched suit and cowboy boots at home. If they wear cowboy boots, saddle up, pardner! If they're sticklers about calling secretaries by their last names, you'd better tell "Jones" to hold your calls during an important meeting. Imitation of executives' pet phrases is an outstanding way to demonstrate your uncontrollable affinity for their habits. It doesn't require extensive wardrobe expense and can be used repeatedly. Pay attention to key phrases; every organization has them and loves to hear its people using them.

Pay careful attention to the way executives in general move and talk. The management in your organization is probably not different from most. One of every executive's primary concerns is to generate the right appearance and image. You'll notice that they never appear to be hurrying, even when they're moving quickly; power and status are associated with having the self-assurance not to hurry or appear impatient. Speak slowly and without excitement in your voice (unless you're rhapsing euphoric about the virtues of the organization; in that case, a somewhat restrained fervor is OK). Important people are viewed as showing even less of their emotions through movement or speech than even the most professional middle manager. I know it's ridiculous, but that's the way it is. Looking rushed, hurried, or upset makes it appear that you are out of control or perhaps having problems handling your work. You don't need to foster that impression even if it's true. Note how heroes in the movies, TV, or literature are always portrayed. No matter how bad the situation— whether it's the fall of the Alamo, the impending bankruptcy of their company, or finding their spouse with the gardener among the rhodo- dendrons—the heroes always keep their cool. It doesn't matter that most chief executives of failing companies are ulcer-ridden. Reality doesn't matter. What matters are the fantasies and expectations that the people at work have. And they have the fantasy that real executives don't show emotion or look harried. Take your time, and look like the calm, unflappable executive you're trying to be.

Walking is a particularly important mannerism that gets very little of the attention it deserves as an image generator. Walking is extremely important to your business image even though it has nothing at all to do with your business savvy or management skills. Nonetheless, how you walk is perceived by many people as a window to your business soul. As outlined above, you don't want to look like you're in a hurry. At the same time, it must appear that you are on your way to something important. Those who see you go by should be left with the impression that you are on your way to confer with top management on a critical issue. Do not saunter along as if you are out for a Sunday stroll; it looks like you're not busy. Be purposeful, but do not rush. Many people who do not follow the other rules seem to follow this one. Unfortunately, most of them equate a thumping military march with the confident stride of an executive.

Slouching, hands in pockets, looking at the floor, a goose-stepping march, or meandering aimlessly are not going to help you look like an executive.

Rule 28: Always evaluate the wisdom of planned actions by imagining the worst possible consequences that could occur.

It's sad that initiative and creativity have been all but snuffed out by committee decision making and the rule of the narrow-minded and timid. It's sad, but that's the way it is. There are only a few organizations that truly value risk taking and view honest, potentially successful failures as learning experiences. If you work for one of these organizations, you'll know it. If you have any doubts at all, you don't. Don't be fooled or misled by management's appeals to your emotions in regard to taking chances and not being afraid of failure. Such exhortations are just meaningless pap for the annual report, speeches, or the newsletter. For example, a particular quote from Teddy Roosevelt is often used in management development seminars to incite managers to take reasonable risks in pursuing creative approaches:

Far better it is to dare mighty things, to win glorious triumphs, even though checkered by failure, than to take rank with those poor spirits who neither enjoy much nor suffer much, because they live in the gray twilight that knows not victory or defeat.

Bully for Teddy. It's sad to say, but he wouldn't even be able to win a congressional seat with that approach these days. Very often, people who make it to the top will contend that they did it by taking desperate chances and incredible risks. Maybe a few did. However, most of the time it's just empty bragging and self-delusion. And for every one who did make it by taking chances, there are hundreds of others who failed with the same technique. If you're in an organization that truly rewards Teddy's recommended approach, go for it! If you're not, you'll find that the rewards for risk taking will be small. If you're successful in spite of the organizational inertia you'll have to overcome, you'll get little credit for your sacrifices. You'll make a lot of jealous enemies who will tone down the benefits of what you've done, management will cluck over the fact that you had to step on a few toes, and the majority of the process protectors will be angry at you for creating more work for them. And if you're unsuccessful, you'll find that the failure will be punished swiftly and horribly. Most organizations do not have reward systems for creativity and extraordinary effort. All you'll get for going the extra mile is sore feet. A consistent low profile is your goal.

Rule 29: Learn peoples' names, and use them as much as you can.

People like to be recognized. When you greet them by name, they feel special. Learn the names of all the brass you are likely to encounter in your facility, and greet them by name when you see them. The same goes for secretaries of executives. A little politeness will go far with them. All it takes is one "That Ms. Smith is such a polite, professional young lady" from some senior secretary to the president, and you could have the edge you need to ace out one of your peers for the next promotion. Every little bit helps.

Don't worry if you occasionally forget someone's name. When in doubt, omit the name, smile a lot, and just use the greeting. Also very useful in establishing yourself as a polite, concerned professional is to inquire about some item of information from a previous encounter. If their spouse was ill, ask in passing, "And how is your husband/wife?" Keep it general and superficial. These types of inquiries will demonstrate the appearance of concern for them as unique individuals. In your greetings, avoid such things as "How are ya?" or "Nice to see ya."

Stick to the more formal-sounding "Good morning," "Good evening," or "Good afternoon." They sound more formal, cool, and distant (professional) to those who count.

Rule 30: Always be as friendly, sympathetic, and understanding as is appropriate.

You can get into just as much trouble by being too friendly and understanding as you can by being arrogant. If someone has a death in the family, give them your sincere condolences and arrange to have the standard organization card or flowers sent to them. If someone has a child who is graduating from college, congratulate them. If someone has a family problem, express your concern if they tell you about it. In the following example, Mary demonstrates the correct technique.

Mary: "Ralph, I hear that your daughter is about to graduate from college. You must be very proud."

Ralph: "Oh, yes!...."

Mary (at Ralph's first pause for a breath): "Well, please give her my congratulations. Now, have you had a chance to look over this proposal?"

Neat, clean, crisp, quick, and back to work—just the right impression. You must appear to be a caring, feeling person. On the other hand, do not become a crying towel for the department's problems, as Fred demonstrates in the following example.

Fred (seeking out Ralph): "Oh, Ralph, I heard that your wife has to have an operation. Tell me all about it."

Ralph: "Well, it's just terrible. You know how hospitals and doctors are. Last month...."

Fred is on the hook for a good fifteen minutes of clinical detail that would bore the most dedicated surgical resident. The last thing you need is to become known as "Good Old Freddy—you can always go to him with a problem." Management will not be impressed with your counseling activities. Too much of a bleeding-heart response to peoples' problems by nonprofessionals generally represents a plea for attention on the part of the sympathy giver. Notice how people will ask about another's surgery just so they can then spout off about their own adventures under the knife. If you find yourself playing the same type of game, give it some serious thought. Chances are that you're not getting enough strokes to keep you happy. If that's the case, work on improving your personal relationships outside of work. Using fake sympathy to get attention rings hollow, won't get you real strokes, and will make you look like a milksop to management.

If you are carefully following Rules 25 and 72, you will have little trouble minimizing this problem. The impression you want to leave is, "Fred is a good guy, but he's too busy to get very involved." When that gets around to top management, it can only help (they all think they're too busy to be nice, too).

Rule 31: Never leave work right at quitting time, and always arrive a little early.

Careful adherence to this rule can have tremendous impact. This is largely because of the fact that hardly anybody seems to get to work on time anymore. And at the end of the day in most organizations, it's life-threatening to stand near the door when the stampede starts thirty minutes before the official quitting time. Once when I was trying to sell some consulting work to a government agency, I attended a meeting that began at 2:00 P.M. Official quitting time was 4:15. By 3:00, the squirming on the part of the attendees was frenzied as they (all senior-level staffers) began to realize that the meeting might run to 3:30 or even 4:00, thus threatening to cut into their customary early departure times. All of a sudden, they began to get up and leave, each in turn mumbling something about another meeting that they had to attend and for which they were late. By 3:15, my colleague and I were the only ones left in the room. Even the division director had left "to go to another meeting." As we were driving out of the parking lot at 3:30, we saw almost all of the attendees walking to their cars. Even in that hopeless situation, you could build a reputation as a hard worker by just sticking around until quitting time (as long as you didn't "rub it in"). You must always give management the impression that you can barely contain your urge to be at work all the time. Showing up a little early and leaving a little late will create that impression.

Rule 32: Never precipitate a meeting or action when you are angry.

Your success depends on careful rule following and consistency. When your emotions are in control, you are going to do things that are, at best, out of character for your rule-generated image or, at worst, will offend or anger someone of consequence (which could be anybody in the organization; you never know who will say something to someone important). The problem with anger is that it will get you into trouble even when you're right. You may be right, but the wisest course in a particular situation might be just to forget the whole thing. If you fly off the handle in moral outrage over the fact that somebody bought a desk without corporate approval, you may get the criminal in trouble, but the bad taste you leave in everybody's mouth over the whole affair may cause you problems later. ("Well, I think she could handle the job, but she always seems to be the center of controversy. I think we need someone more diplomatic.") Remember the old adage about counting to ten when you get angry? Well, do it, and then forget about what happened until the next day. If you must flash off the blistering memo, write it out in longhand and put it away for a few days. Do not complain about the situation to anyone (Rule 23). Trust me; it's not as important as it seems. Take a moment, and think of the immensity of the universe, the billions of stars, the thousands of advanced civilizations out there. Think of the hundreds of "crises" you've had in your life that, in retrospect, seem trivially unimportant. Now, does it still seem so bad that Lloyd dumped on your proposal? Of course not.

Rule 33: Always keep your work area Spartan, clean, and organized.

I personally enjoy offices with plants, fish tanks, and art work. But then again, few psychologists get to be presidents of big organizations. Anything more than a minimal amount of personal effects in an office tends to leave the impression that you are not busy enough. The idea that you could occasionally have the time to look up from your desk to enjoy your surroundings is disconcerting to some people. If your office is overdecorated (which can mean "tastefully" if you're working with a bunch of drones), crammed with personal mementos, or furnished in nonstandard manner (as if you're the only one in the building with the wicker look), people will think that you are more interested in interior decorating than in the work.

The bigger but more subtle danger is that if you make your office too relaxing and enjoyable, you will relax your vigilance against informality; if it seems more like home, you may start to act more like you do when you are at home. That is, you will begin to act like a reasonable, emotional, not all-gung-ho-for-the-company person. Such behavior at work is very dangerous to your young career. Even worse, if your office is too nice (any nicer than the barren cubicles of your colleagues), other personnel will come by to visit and/or show off your office to guests. You don't need this type of publicity unless you work for an interior decorating company or an architect.

Rule 34: Always maintain the most exceptional physical appearance possible.

The greatest part of all opinions held about you will be directly related to how you look. Remember, most of the people at work, and even in your neighborhood, don't know you very well. But they all know what you look like. They all make assumptions about your unknown or little-known characteristics based upon what they see. Pay attention to this most critical aspect of your overall image. Do not deceive yourself into believing that we have progressed (either as a society or as individuals) so far that we evaluate each other based on inner qualities. Likewise, don't believe that if we don't know someone, we wait until we have enough data before we draw any conclusions. If you hitchhike in a three-piece suit carrying a leather attaché case, you'll get a lot of rides with people who would never pick up someone dressed in a dirty tee-shirt and jeans. You get the point. Physical appearance is critical. Let's face it; if you look different, strange, or exceptional, you're going to get more attention than everyone else. Career-wise, there is good attention and there is bad attention. Do not allow things that generate ''bad'' attention to go unchanged. Keep yourself in the best shape that you can. Overweight people just don't look as energetic as more normally pro-portioned people. People with bloodshot eyes don't appear to be as alert and may be assumed to be having troubles with the work load or alcohol. It doesn't matter at all whether these evaluations are valid. People will latch on to any minor defect and use it to justify any and all half-baked and ill-founded opinions about you.

Take an honest look at yourself, and do what you can to make yourself as physically attractive as possible. If you've got more than normal appearance problems, get some professional help. A little plastic surgery or a hair transplant might make all the difference. Why kill yourself to follow the rules, get all sorts of degrees, work fifty or sixty hours a week, and then compromise any part of the effort because of a neglected physical dimension that could be fixed? You're not the one setting the standards, but even if you don't like them, you're going to be evaluated according to how well you stack up against them.

An often overlooked but very easy way to improve your personal appearance is to smile at all times when encountering other personnel. A smile will make other people feel that you are happy with them and with things in general; they will feel more relaxed and less worried when they are around you. These feelings will be associated with your presence and will lead them to feel good about you. They will be easier to work with and will tend to say good things about you to others. If you are like me, your natural facial expression (when you are not actively flexing any facial muscles) may be interpreted as a scowl. I was shocked once to have a colleague tell me that he knew I was unhappy because I was always scowling. Don't assume that you look happy and friendly just because you feel that way inside. Check out how you look, and make sure that you're flashing what they will call a smile. After you've done it for a while, you'll stop feeling like a smiling, drooling idiot, and you'll be pleasantly surprised to find that people will just naturally smile back at you.

Rule 35: Always dress slightly more conservatively than the norm for your organization.

You always want to look like you're ready for the next management level, so dress the part. Rule 27 briefly mentioned that it's essential to emulate the dress of executives as part of your demonstration of fraternity. Copy their clothing styles, but always be a little more conservative than they are. This will demonstrate that you are a little afraid to loosen up in their presence (which will show them that you respect and recognize their power and status) and that you are on your best behavior because you are eagerly seeking their approval. In most organizations, the dress of executives gets more conservative as they move higher up the corporate ladder. This may be because of the fact that it is difficult in most localities to find less conservative suits on which you can spend $800 a shot. To a certain extent, more expensive wardrobes are viewed as more conservative simply because they cost a lot. If the "uniform" at your level in your organization is a shirt and tie, wear a sportcoat with it. Ignore any ribbing. It will stop after a day or so (in fact, you may generate imitations). If the style in your organization is three-piece suits, wear a watch fob or honorary chain. Since most higher-level executives in the organization won't know much about your work, you'll be allowing them to draw the most favorable conclusions from what they do know about you: your appearance. You'll look like you're ready to join them.

Rule 36: Avoid the use of profanities.

It's not the content of profanities that's the problem. These days everyone is familiar with most of the profanities. The problem is that the use of profanities suggests a loss of control. You must appear to be in control all the time. The use of profanities will add an emotional tone to what you say, even if you're not being emotional. Since many people use profanities only when they get hurt or very angry, your casual use of a profanity may send a false signal that you are angry at them or at the organization. As Rules 18 and 32 pointed out, it is bad news to imply any criticism of anything. A secondary consideration is that a sizable portion of the population views profanities as bad.

You don't need to unknowingly offend someone who is sensitive to the occasional profanity. Play it safe, and hold back on the profanities.

One area in which a carefully planned but spontaneous-appearing exception must be made now and then is when you must talk tough in meetings with the brass. In these encounters, unless you have knowledge of the executives' preferences against such language, you can demonstrate your fervent pro-company emotionality by the use of such phrases as, "Damn it, we don't have to sit back and take this nonsense from XYZ Industries!" Said with a steely, controlled tone, such expressions will be very effective, particularly if you are not known as someone who normally uses such terms. But be careful; know your audience well before you take a chance.

5

Rules for Managing
Peer Relationships at Work

"Mary and I are going to the cafeteria for a cup of coffee. Come on along and the three of us can relax and talk a little."

"Bob, you should see what J.B. did to my department's budget! He really murdered me. How did you do?"

"I'm meeting Fred and Lloyd for a few drinks after work. We're going to talk over the problem we're having with Priscilla. Want to join us?"

"Diana, this is Mary. Look, I just found out about the reorganization. Our two departments are taking all the flak. We have to talk."

"Bob, this is John. The meeting is set for this afternoon at three. Say, did you hear the news? I just heard that Jones is having an affair with that fox Cassandra in contracts. Can you believe it?!"

"Hey, Sally, how's it going? I suppose you've heard they finally got rid of Johnson. It sure took them long enough!"

These read like transcripts from Typical Business, Inc., of Everytown, USA. You no doubt hear these or their equivalents every day in your organization. If you listen to such statements with an ear attuned to the rules, you'll hear something much different: the unmistakable sounds of people trying to flush their careers down the toilet. Statements such as the above generally occur between peers. Peers are members of the organization who perceive one another as being at about the same level of responsibility, authority, pay, status, promotional opportunities, and so on. As a result of their perceived common characteristics, peers have a strong tendency to identify with one another. This provides support and comfort to the individuals in the group. Part of this support and comfort comes from the exchange of mutual confidences.

67

All of this is perfectly natural social behavior for human beings. Once again, I must reiterate that so-called natural social behaviors are the kiss of death to your success at work. If you were working as a food gatherer and grub hunter in a primitive tribe, such social behaviors would prove invaluable in establishing and maintaining the group cohesion necessary for individual survival.

In a more typical work environment, such group cohesion and the behaviors it encourages are bad news without exception. Peers are the second biggest danger to your career after bosses. As with bosses, you have no choice but to interact with peers on a daily basis. If you follow the rules in this chapter, you'll run into few problems (of your own creation) with peers.

Rule 37: Do not make friends with your peers.

This is one of the most difficult rules to follow. Rule 25 asserts that you cannot safely relax and get personal with fellow employees. The situation is even more dangerous when peers are involved. It seems natural to get friendly with the people who face the same obstacles every day and with whom you probably interact on a daily basis. Well, being natural isn't going to get you to the top. You are at work to further your career and to get the job done, in that order. If you need to make friends, join a club, but do not make friends at work, and especially not with peers. They are the ones you're going to have to fight with for the next rung on the corporate ladder. They have the most to gain if you fail. Every peer you confide in becomes a sharp dagger poised at the soft, white underbelly of your success in the organization. Each of your peers has a constantly changing set of fears, insecurities, and needs. You never know what they'll need in the future or how badly they'll think they need it. Given the right set of circumstances, one of your peers may feel that your personal confidences are a tool for them to use for their own purposes. Even if they're trying to help you, they can cause serious damage, which your career can't afford.

John: "Well, J.B., that's about it. I think we've got a good chance to get the proposal in by June 15."

J.B.: "Very good, very good. Now, who are we going to send back east to head up the negotiation team? It should be someone familiar with the Washington area and someone who has worked with the government contracting process before."

John: "How about Fred? He worked as a senior contracts type with

Acme Industries back in D.C. As a matter of fact, he just got back from spending a week in D.C. visiting family.''

J.B.: ''Very interesting. I'll keep him in mind.''

What J.B. will keep in mind is that Fred had told him that he was going to spend the week at an executive development seminar and industry group meeting in Boston. Fred had confided the truth in John because John was a peer and could be trusted. Fred had been exchanging confidences as part of his peer group's cohesion maintenance activities. The result is that Fred is in big trouble. It doesn't help that John really was trying to help. In his enthusiasm to get the assignment for Fred, John forgot that Fred had told him that he was supposed to be in Boston. If a well-meaning peer can do this to Fred, think what a back-stabber could do on purpose. Your peers are your competitors on the organizational ladder; you can't be friends with someone whose face you may have to step on to get to the next rung. They won't hesitate if they look down and see that your face is their only foothold.

Rule 38: Do not join cliques of any kind.

You cannot afford to align yourself with any one group. Further, you can't afford to be perceived as being a member of any one group. You must be perceived as your own person, who just happens to be a company person. When you are perceived as being part of a clique, you are automatically assumed to possess some of that clique's characteristics. This would not be a problem if each and every member of the clique was an expert rule follower; there would be no unfavorable characteristics for you to be associated with. Every clique is comprised of members drawn from the organization as a whole. As such, every clique has a significant number of idiots, troublemakers, and malcontents. It is extremely dangerous to associate your business image with the general impression that such a motley group creates among the organization's other members.

Another drawback to clique membership is the fact that you can never be sure of how the fortunes of a clique will go. Even a clique that is solidly aligned with a successful executive presents dangers to its members. If the executive leaves the organization, the clique members will be unprotected from any vengeance moves by those who suffered or perceived that they suffered at the hands of the clique. A compounding problem is that once a clique is formed, its members begin to get a little reckless, thinking that the clique will protect them or reduce their visibility when the clique does something nasty. As a result of this unrealistic delusion, clique members often do things that get other organization members very angry. Since most cliques are merely loose social groups without any formal ties to an executive, individual members get no help when they are called to task for clique-inspired behaviors. Even if there is executive membership in the clique, that's no guarantee of protection. Few executives will put themselves at risk to try to increase profits if it requires unpopular action. They certainly won't risk anything to bail you out just because you got carried away by clique social pressures. And if the protecting executive moves on to another organization, the clique members will find that they have few allies. Spurn cliques like the plague; they will only cause you trouble.

Rule 39: Identify and associate with the organization's rising stars, golden ones, and acclaimed winners.

This is not a refutation of or exception to Rule 38. The purpose of this rule is to allow you to absorb as much positive image as you can without doing anything of substance. Fortunately for you, proximity to something favorable will generally result in your being perceived as favorable just because you're in the area. You want the casual and not so casual observer to come to the conclusion that the "golden ones" are an important part of your usual professional contacts. You want everyone to assume that you participate in the decision making and that your input is important to the movers and shakers. They will come to all of these conclusions simply on the basis of mere (and properly orchestrated) proximity. If you can have lunch in the middle of the executive dining room or the company cafeteria with the current top salesperson, do it. If you get the chance to serve on a committee with some of the real movers and shakers, serve. If your organization's golden ones participate in a lot of company sporting activities, it's time to get in there and win one for J.B. Don't join teams that don't have a lot of top management members if sports are a big thing around the boardroom.

There are dangers here that you must be careful about. Do not join a clique of these people; simply be seen with them once in a while. Do not relax your constant vigilance with them; they will chew you up and spit you out like day-old gum at the first opportunity. And don't press too hard to get close to the golden ones if you're getting a lot of resistance. If you push, they'll see you as a leech, and you'll get treated and talked about like dirt. It'll take a little time to get close, and it'll take even more time if you're several levels beneath them in the hierarchy.

Rule 40: Regularly solicit technical advice and assistance from your peers.

Since you aren't going to be trying to make friends with your peers at work (Rule 37) and you won't be exchanging confidences with your employees (Rule 72), the organization is going to have to form its impression of you on the basis of your interactions with its members as you do your job. Encounters with your peers can be your best tools for this purpose. Use your day-to-day job responsibilities to create a very positive impression among them and any observers. You can do this by always giving the impression that you are eagerly seeking the assistance of your peers, particularly those whose opinions are most important to your success. It's strange but true that people will like you more if they help you than if you help them. So give them all a chance to help you. You'll be seen as a real team player and someone who is safely intelligent (sharp enough to know you should ask them but not smart enough to do without them). Even if they are total idiots, ask them. They'll love you the most. Even if they have nothing to do with the project you're asking about, they'll gladly and gratefully give you help. Expressions like the following are useful:

"Say, Ms. Jacobs, I was just wondering if you could give me some input on this utilization review." (Ms. Jacobs has nothing to do with utilization, but she'll be glad she was asked.)

"Bob, you're just the guy I'm looking for. I'm working on this automated production line design, and I need a fresh perspective. Do you have a few minutes to help me out?" (Bob is a corporate policies and procedures type who hasn't even walked through manufacturing, much less knowing anything about automated production. Nevertheless, he'll be flattered that he was asked.)

"Carol, J.B. said that you're the expert on long-term debentures. Can you give me some advice on this funding report?" (Actually, you know that Carol is a total incompetent whose financial expertise is limited to balancing her checkbook, but she'll be glad she was asked, and she'll say good things about the person who asked her.)

"Fred, I'm glad I caught you before you left. I've got a real problem here, and I need your help. I understand you went to a top school for your MBA. I'm sure they covered financial projections using nondeterministic models. Can you give me some pointers on this forecast?'' (Fred is a typical airhead jargon-spouter whose only familiarity with models derives from a date he had with one three years ago. Nevertheless, Fred will be grateful for the opportunity to hold forth as an expert on the subject.)

After they finish making their learned contributions, thank them (always being careful to keep a straight face), and then ignore what they said. You may occasionally stumble across something of value in their contributions, but the real value in asking them will be the positive press they'll generate about you.

Rule 41: Never discuss salaries.

One of the few eternal truths in the universe is that we always think that everybody else is getting more money than we are. An accompanying corollary is that we feel that we aren't getting what we deserve while everyone else is getting more than they're worth. Take my word for it; the salaries of most of the people you envy are not as high as you think (except the executives; they're getting more).

In my middle management days, a fellow was recruited for a newly created VP of Marketing job. He was given a plush office right next to the executive VP (many managers thought this location was an asset rather than a dangerous liability; see Rule 46), some of the division's best people, and what we all figured had to be a salary of $50,000 or $60,000 plus bonus and car. Everyone was particularly incensed about the salary because there were a number of managers who had wanted the job and would have been willing to do it for less. On top of that, the guy was a real drone, nice but not too sharp. I found out two years later, through the loose lips of an unscrupulous headhunter, that the poor guy had only been getting $30,000, much less than all of us who had been complaining. No wonder he was a drone; you get what you pay for. Yet it had looked like he was getting big bucks. Personnel surveys repeatedly demonstrate that this type of salary inflation about what others earn is common. Save yourself the trouble, and don't worry about it or discuss it. It foments dissent, will depress you for no good reason, and leaves you open to problems if someone says you made a statement about someone else's wages.

Rule 42: Identify and avoid troublemakers at all costs.

Here we are speaking of the complainers, obstructionists, on-the-job retirees, and malcontents who comprise a good proportion of every organization. These people are just looking for one of your loose edges so they can show that you're just as flawed as they are. Since they don't do any work themselves, they keep busy by interfering with the few real workers and by trying to bring everyone down to their own low levels of performance. To these frustrated people, nothing is ever good or OK. Everything is a problem or will be in time. Avoid these people at all costs. If they begin to think that you are the least bit in agreement with any of their negative philosophies about the organization, they will be all over you. They will begin to suggest to others that you are one of them, they will start to drop by your office to visit, and they will begin to quote you in arguments with others. Your success in the organization will suffer an ugly and slow death.

Once this process starts, you can't turn it back. You can't defend yourself without creating even more negative publicity. If you have trouble avoiding these people, such as when you have to work or share an office with one of them, don't be afraid to appear to be brutally frank with them. (You must never actually be frank, but the appearance of it can be useful.) Choke back your gorge and say something like, "Look, Lloyd, I know what your opinions are, but I think this is one swell organization, and I don't think it helps when you run it down all the time." Repeat this as often as necessary. You can't very well be hurt if that type of corn gets around (remember that all of the executives already believe it).

Rule 43: Never admit to anyone that you are angry, depressed, bored, overworked, underworked, or underappreciated.

It's only natural to be tired, angry, or depressed occasionally. Just don't tell anyone at work how you feel. No matter what you say or how innocent it is, it's going to end up hurting you. For example, Fred has just worked sixty-five hours straight with only ten hours of sleep. He bumps into Ralph at the coffee machine, and Ralph asks him why he looks so tired.

Poor tired Fred: "Man, am I beat! I was on a plane all weekend trying to get the Jenkins deal sold, and then I got called in Sunday night to take care of the Williams bid that J.B. wanted to take with him this morning. Sometimes I wonder if it's all worth it.''

Fred was just looking for a little well-deserved sympathy and perhaps an "attaboy" from Ralph. Ralph demonstrates his understanding of the sacrifices that business sometimes requires by his response.

Ralph: "Yeah, I'm beat, too. I had to get here fifteen minutes early today to chair the bowling club breakfast in the cafeteria. I know how you feel.''

Everybody else thinks they're making the ultimate sacrifice, too. So forget about getting your strokes from anyone at work. If you can't give them to yourself, ask at home. Aside from the uselessness of asking at work, you'll expose yourself to some damaging bad press. In the above example, Ralph, if he is as big a troublemaker as he is a lazy bum, will now be able to tell all who will listen that "Fred said sometimes it's not worth it to work for J.B." or "Fred said that sometimes his work load is too much." Fred doesn't need that kind of sympathy or help. Neither do you. That's what real friends and families are for.

Rule 44: Be a booster for everything the organization does.

Every organization has a number of sacred cows that are not directly related to the work itself but are an integral part of the organization's identity in the eyes of the executives. These pet projects and interests are usually nothing but thinly veiled excuses for the organization's brass to get a lot of attention and publicity while you do all the work. As laughable or hypocritical as these projects may seem to the rational observer, you'd better crank up your enthusiasm and give the appearance that you too are 100 percent behind every program. If the organization is pushing the annual charity drive, you had better try and pump money out of your $200-a-week clerks with just as much relish as the chief executive demonstrates by wolfing down caviar at the $1000-per-plate kickoff dinner the company paid for. A smart manager would demonstrate enthusiasm as follows.

Smart manager (to assembled department): "Okay, everyone, listen up. As you know, it's time for the annual charity drive. Now, J.B. is behind this program 100 percent, and I'm behind it 150 percent. I expect all of you to help us make this program a great success for ABC Company.''

Instead of playing it smart like the above manager, a lot of managers would say things along the lines of the following.

Not-so-smart manager: "Well, everyone, it's time for J.B.'s annual pet charity extortion *(snicker, snicker).* I know nobody has much money, and I don't really care if you give or not, but we have to go through the motions. So give *(snicker, chuckle)."*

It's scary just being in the general area of someone ruining their career in that manner. You can almost hear the pink slip typing itself if J.B. hears about it. Remember, there is no distinction in anyone's eyes between your job-related and non-job-related behaviors at the office. It's all your behavior, and it's all being continuously evaluated. Keep it positive and enthusiastic at all times and on all subjects.

Rule 45: Do not offer or react to opinions about anything.

Once you offer an opinion or agree or disagree with someone else's opinion about the looks, sex life, emotional stability, work output, ethnic background, or habits of another person, you are creating serious risks for your career. It's just as dangerous as humor. Even the most innocent opinion or reaction from you can be purposely or inadvertently used against you. For example, Fred runs into Ralph again at the coffee machine (the areas around coffee machines are responsible for more dead careers than bosses). As usual, Ralph is angry at the organization, the world, and himself.

Ralph: "Hi, Fred. Boy, did you see what that idiot J.B. did to the bowling league finals schedule by moving up the date for the new product rollout? What a complete idiot!"

A fast-thinking, rule-following Fred would respond as follows.

Smart Fred: "Well, Ralph, I think J.B. is doing a fine job, and he realizes that the timing of the rollout is more important than the bowling finals."

A stupid Fred wouldn't be that clever.

Stupid Fred: "Well, Ralph, maybe J.B. was just having a bad day and forgot about the bowling finals."

Stupid Fred responded this way because he didn't want to get Ralph angry out of some misplaced and stupid fear that Ralph might not be his friend anymore. But who needs a friend like Ralph anyway? There are plenty of well-adjusted people around to talk with. Even Fred's rather harmless statement will soon be reported to Ralph's beer-drinking bowling cronies as "Even Fred, J.B.'s right-hand man, thinks J.B. was off-base in moving the sales meeting." Fred will be hard pressed to defend himself to J.B. if J.B. hears about it; any denials would just create more ill will. Even worse, J.B. might hear it and never even bring it up to Fred; he'd just start to reduce his trust in Fred. Stick to the tried and true, tired, dry, self-serving, mealy-mouthed company line for all of your opinions and reactions. If there is no company line on a topic, it's a good clue that you shouldn't say anything at all. Remember, people will seldom invent total lies about what you say and do, but they will embroider and misinterpret the least little thing with great enthusiasm. Don't give them the chance.

6

Rules for Managing Your Bosses

The worst thing that can happen to a career is a boss (and your employees feel likewise about your effect on their careers). The problem is that while bosses are the biggest hazard you face, you have no choice but to interact with them on a daily or hourly basis. The key to successful boss management is to manage the interactions to your best possible advantage while minimizing the potential danger. It's not easy. Sometimes things will work out badly with your boss no matter what you do. If, despite the use of this chapter's rules, your boss is still creating a lot of extraordinary problems for you (almost all bosses continually create unextraordinary problems for their employees; this is normal and expected), you'd better take a close look at other areas of your work behavior. It could be that you're not handling your employees correctly and they're whining to your boss (who is listening), or maybe you're blowing it on general demeanor issues. If you're sure it's not you who is causing the problems (it usually is), perhaps you have a defective boss.

It's no secret that a lot of socially inept, intellectually limited, disorganized, and nasty people find their way into management. If you're saddled with one of the more hopeless versions of these disasters, you have two choices:

1. You can hang on and see if things will change. The odds are not in your favor. Organizations and people can't change very much in a given period of time and won't change at all if they're comfortable with the situation. And blind luck probably won't help much. If you do decide to hang in there a little longer, make sure you put the time to good use by obeying all of the rules.

77

2. You can move your career to another location and try again. The biggest problem with this approach is that people give up too soon and leave before they've given the situation a chance by carefully applying the rules. Or they expect too much out of a job in general and are seeking something they won't ever find because it doesn't exist.

The boss–employee relationship is particularly treacherous because there's a large dose of mastery and subservience in it. In such a critical situation, you'll make a lot of serious mistakes if you follow your natural emotional inclinations while you're engaged in heavy-duty boss-manipulation activities. Emotions may help if you're trying to outrun the proverbial saber-toothed tiger, but they won't help you maintain your career's consciousness while your bosses have their thumbs on your career's carotid artery. It will be incredibly difficult to be objective in all of your boss-management activities, but the rules will show you how. It will be worth the effort. If you do it well, both your career and that of your boss will prosper.

Rule 46: Always minimize your contact with your boss.

This is the most important rule for properly managing your boss. Even if you break all of the other boss-management rules, observance of this one will minimize the damage. Avoidance of the boss at every opportunity seems to run counter to a lot of workers' natural inclinations. After all, they reason, shouldn't you try to get the boss to notice you as much as possible? No way; stay out of your boss's way as much as you can. Get your work done as well as necessary (too well can be just as bad as not well enough), follow the rules in this section, and then avoid your boss at every opportunity. You perceive your boss from a very narrow perspective: yours. Your boss has innumerable other things to worry about that involve his or her personal life, other employees, bosses, career, and so on. The last thing on his or her mind is a detailed concern for the minutiae of how your day is going. What your boss wants is to have things in general go as smoothly as possible with a minimum of interruptions, embarrassments, problems, and surprises. He or she doesn't want to be bothered by unnecessary daily or hourly visits that are nothing but your thinly veiled ploys to get attention. An intelligent boss has no difficulty perceiving the difference between the legitimate business call from a subordinate and a "Hey, boss, here I am again, looking for strokes" meeting. The boss won't appreciate being bothered in order to participate in your ego-maintenance activities. A stupid boss may not realize what's going on but is even more dangerous. The stupid boss will always be in a state of confused turmoil as he or she attempts to manage the mess he or she has made. This boss will be flailing around for anything that will help. The only reward you'll get from hanging around this type of boss will be more of someone else's work.

Unnecessary visits to the boss are dangerous for another reason. You can never be sure of how the boss will react to what you present because you can never be completely aware of all the other influences that have been at work before your visit. You may get an unpleasant surprise. On the other hand, if your boss initiates the contact by summoning you, you can be more reasonably assured that the encounter will at least start off with issues that are related to your work. When you initiate more contacts with the boss than the boss requires to get his or her job done, you run the risk of getting more of someone else's work to do, irritating the boss, and/or having the boss bring up something that you're not prepared to deal with. Avoid your boss as much as possible. Everybody will be happier.

Rule 47: Regularly let your boss know how impressed you are by his or her work load.

Bosses are just like other workers; most of them are limited in intellect and creativity. And, just like most other workers, many of them don't have much to do. Yet they all think they're overworked and strained to the limits of human endurance. They feel overworked and underappreciated. Take advantage of this misconception and use it to your advantage. Let your boss know that you recognize the heavy load he or she shoulders. Let your boss know that you are awed by it. Lines such as "I don't know how you do it" and "Your work load is amazing; I don't know what we'd do if anything ever happened to you" are particularly useful if you can keep a straight face. Of course, you must be subtle and selective in how and where you attempt this type of shameless groveling. Many bosses occasionally feel guilty about how little they do. When they are in this condition, it is dangerous to call attention to or heighten their guilt. Their response would be to blame you for their vague feelings of discomfort rather than to do anything constructive such as some work.

Fortunately for you, bosses usually will signal when they want a few strokes by saying things like "Look at this desk; I can't find a thing" or "I worked all weekend on the Jenkins deal." When you hear this type of whining, go for it.

Rule 48: Do not get friendly or personal with your boss.

You are obviously dependent upon your boss for many things such as challenging work, good performance reviews, and salary increases. Given this dependency, you must fight hard to resist the temptation to cultivate a personal relationship with your boss. This tendency to become friendly, even with a boss who isn't particularly nice, demonstrates the operation of an ego defense mechanism that Freudian psychologists call reaction formation. It works in the following way. You resent your boss's power over you and are uncomfortable with the implications of admitting your weakness. At the same time, you have to give the appearance of being nice to him or her if you want to get ahead. Your subconscious reduces the conflict by saying, "Hey, if I'm being nice to this person, he or she must deserve it, because I'm not a hypocrite." You can short-circuit this process by being objective with yourself about your boss at all times. If your boss gets to know you personally, his or her perceptions of your personal life will color his or her work-related views of you. You don't need that kind of sewage clouding up the crystal-clear waters of your carefully filtered business image.

Even if you're not volunteering such data, your boss may occasionally get fairly aggressive in trying to dig some personal information out of you. Often, a boss will solicit personal information in order to reassure himself or herself that you, and others, are having the same types of personal problems that he or she is experiencing. Or the boss may simply want to dredge up your problems to make his or her own seem smaller. Some older bosses like to hear about the personal problems of their workers on the misguided assumption that they can offer helpful advice. None of these reasons is valid or appropriate at work. All are dangerous. Any flaws you admit will become part of the overall impression you generate at work. You'll have enough trouble simply generating an overall positive impression in a neutral environment. If your boss is really pressing for some personal disclosures and you think he or she might get irritated if you don't play the game, keep them as general and innocent as you can. For example, Fred is in a meeting with J.B. Just as Fred is about to leave, J.B. tries to dredge up the slops on Fred's personal life.

J.B.: "Tell me, Fred, you have a teenage son at home, don't you?"

Fred: "Yes, sir, I do. Freddy Jr. is sixteen."

J.B.: "Well, I don't know what I'm going to do with J.B. II. He got drunk last night and wrecked the new Ferrari that his grandmother bought him. It's only the fourth car he's wrecked, and I suppose anyone could get arrested three or four times for drunk driving in a year, but, still, I'm worried about him."

J.B. pauses expectantly, waiting for Fred to ante up a similar problem so that J.B. will feel better. Fred remains crafty.

Fred: "That's a shame, J.B. It's probably just one of those isolated mistakes that everyone makes now and then. Maybe it's just a phase."

J.B. now feels a little isolated. He sees that Fred isn't going to help him out by complaining about Freddy Jr. Nevertheless, J.B. gives it one more try.

J.B.: "Well, yes, I see. I suppose you've had similar troubles with your boy, huh?"

Fred keeps it professional and positive.

Fred: "Well, we've been very fortunate. Freddy Jr. has been lucky so far to avoid problems. Of course, we're keeping our fingers crossed as he approaches college."

Fred refuses to serve up the personal slops, but he's wise enough not to rub it in by mentioning that Freddy Jr. is a National Merit Scholarship winner, an Eagle Scout, owner of his own software development company, and a national karate champion. Besides, as J.B. should realize, such personal details are not a work-related item. (They're dangerous even if they're overwhelmingly positive, as this case should demonstrate.) J.B. gives up.

J.B.: "Well, it's nice to hear that Freddy Jr. is doing well. I'll see you at the meeting on Monday."

J.B. is a little disgruntled because Fred wouldn't help him with his guilt-management activities, but he probably doesn't realize why he's irritated. Fred's refusal to serve up the slops just makes him look better in J.B.'s eyes even if J.B. is not actively aware of his perceptions. Fred's apparent mastery of his home life only makes him seem more in charge at work. Do not serve up any garbage. It's better to risk causing a little jealous irritation by appearing not to have any big problems than to run your dirty linen up the flagpole in public.

The only safe approach is to view your boss as a part of the organization that you must carefully regulate, monitor, manipulate, and control (relative to your needs) in order to succeed. View your boss as a strange, dangerous, and unpredictable physical object whose controls are unfamiliar. If you lose this perspective, you are asking for trouble.

Rule 49: Always convey to your boss the impression that you believe that his or her department is the most important one in the organization.

It's natural for people to think that their department is the most important one in the organization. They identify more closely with their own small work group than with the organization as a whole. This strong identification with their day-to-day work group leads them to aggressively defend, support, and perpetuate the norms and roles of the small group with a fervor they'll never show for the organization as a whole. The people in the mail room think that they keep everything going, the secretaries think that they are the only ones who know what is going on (in many organizations, this is true), and the cleaning crew thinks that the whole system would collapse if the executive washroom was not cleaned regularly. Since this universal phenomenon is even stronger among insecure and narrow-minded people like your boss, you can use it to your advantage. Your boss and most of the others in your department already think that their department is the center of the organization's universe. If you display contrary or less than enthusiastic support for this notion than others in your group, you'll get a lot of negative attention. The situation in regard to bosses is even more sensitive. Bosses are always struggling to justify their budgets and policies. Anything you can do to ease their doubts and fears about their own importance will be invaluable in establishing a positive perception of yourself in their eyes. If you do not help them shore up their pitiful fears and doubts, they will view it not just as a lack of the support they expect as their right but as a direct attack on them. You'll be in big trouble.

Rule 50: Regularly thank your boss for all the guidance, support, and direction that he or she has been giving you.

Good bosses always feel guilty that they don't give enough support even if they do. Bad bosses always think their occasional mere presence is sufficient to inspire the troops. When you thank a good boss, you reduce his or her guilt level and are perceived positively. Lines such as "Manufacturing (or whatever department you're in) is what this company is all about" are useful both in direct interactions with the boss and as indirect comments to other workers that will eventually reach the boss's ear. When you thank a terrible boss for nonexistent support, you reap several benefits. Bad bosses are usually harboring a lot of guilt over their sorry performance levels. A few strokes from you will help them keep their guilt under control; they'll appreciate your help. Further, the bad boss will perceive you as a more astute underling than his or her other employees because most of them will be venting their hatred by not giving these types of clever strokes. As a result, you'll look even better by comparison. Universally effective expressions include such pap as:

"J.B., I want you to know that I appreciate the guidance and direction you've been providing."

"Ms. Jacobs, I really can't express my thanks enough for the great help you've given me in getting this report into shape."

"Boss, I want you to know that I've never worked for anyone who has made it as easy for me to do a good job. I really appreciate it."

Until you become practiced in this technique, it is not wise to attempt it on a full stomach; it's enough to make anyone sick. In fact, periods of illness are great times to try this ploy; your pained expression will be seen as filial respect. Don't get reckless and try the above expressions if you're in a playful mood. One smile or smirk, and your boss, however stupid or slow, will realize what you're doing.

Rule 51: Never argue with your boss about anything.

You can't win. Once the boss has strongly stated a position or has made up his or her mind, he or she is not going to change it no matter what you do. All arguing does is create ill will and damage the boss's perception of you as a pleasant, intelligent worker. At the first sign of a negative reaction from your boss, back off immediately and terminate the meeting as soon as diplomatically possible. You want to cut short the amount of time the boss associates you with a disagreement or emotional distress. For example, note the following interaction.

Ms. Jacobs: "Damn it, Fred, I'm not sure I understand what you're trying to do with this proposal to reorganize the Contracts department."

Fred should recognize the boss's "damn it" as a danger sign.

Fred: "Well, I think we can increase productivity 20 percent if we shuffle responsibilities like I've shown in the chart."

Ms. Jacobs: "Damn it, Fred, don't you see that Johnson will have to manage two more people? He's already stretched to the limit!"

Johnson is a pet of the boss. It is immaterial that Johnson is a lazy incompetent; his groveling skills are legend. Fred must deal with the real world if this situation is to be salvaged. If Fred had planned ahead, he would have designed his proposal so that Johnson would get more title, more money, and less work. And if that arrangement wouldn't increase productivity, Fred should look for safer projects. As it is, Fred recognizes that the boss is starting to get polarized and may forbid further work on the project if the discussion turns into an argument. Fred does the smart thing.

Fred: "You're absolutely right, Priscilla. It was foolish of me to overlook that. Johnson pumps out his work so well that some of us assume that he can do anything. Let me take this proposal home and work on it a little more. Oh, before I leave, have you had time to review the proposed colors for the softball team uniforms?"

This is a good exit. The boss was flattered, suitably mollified, and then moved on to a nonthreatening and pleasant topic. Fred managed a quick recovery and escape from a situation that a novice might have turned into an ugly scene.

Rule 52: Never attempt to defend yourself when the boss is reprimanding you.

When your boss begins to criticize or reprimand you for a real or perceived error, don't fight it. Let your boss finish the tirade and then quickly and humbly admit your error. Follow this with an assurance that it won't happen again because you'll be trying harder. Then get out of there as quickly as you can. Unless you are being wrongly accused of a monstrous error or crime that could get you fired, you can't win by defending yourself. It will only make your boss angrier. It is far better to just cut the whole thing off by admitting your error and promising to do better. This will take the wind out of your boss's sails. A large part of a boss's anger in this type of situation is his or her perception that you are going to react emotionally, get upset, and create an unpleasant scene. This gets the boss even more keyed up ahead of time. If you don't fight back, the boss is relieved and will have a much more positive impression of you. For example, consider the following attitude adjustment session in which J.B. is chastising Joan because there were some typos on a big mailer that went out. Joan is in charge of the Graphic Arts department at ABC Company.

Joan: "You wanted to see me, J.B.?"

J.B.: "Yes, Joan. We have a very serious problem here. Last week, these two brochures went out to 75,000 customers with a number of typos on them. *We can't afford this type of bad PR*"

Joan: "Yes, this is a serious problem, J.B., but my department isn't responsible." (An admission of guilt here would have defused a large part of J.B.'s anger. Instead, Joan is not only validating J.B.'s fears of a bad scene, but she's actually telling him he's incorrect in his assignment of the blame.)

J.B. (now really angry): "Well, who the hell's fault is it, then? Your people design the brochures, don't they? The damn Maintenance department doesn't do them, *do they?*"

Joan: "Yes, sir. We do them all right, but we don't send them to the printer until we get a signoff from the Marketing department. As far as I know, we never got the signoff. I didn't even release them to the printer."

J.B.: "Signoff? *Signoff?* Joan, I'm talking about our *image*. The image that my father, Big J.B., spent his whole life building. I'm talking about reputation, image, customer respect. *I don't want to hear about signoffs!* How could this happen?"

J.B. now knows (or at least suspects) that Joan probably isn't responsible for the screw-up, but he'd never admit it, not even to himself. This makes him feel guilty for both losing control and blaming the wrong person. More fatal to what's left of Joan's career, J.B. has experienced a very traumatic session, and he'll associate the whole thing with Joan. Every time he sees her, his blood pressure will go up a little, and he'll feel a little embarrassed and guilty. Those feelings aren't going to do Joan's career any good. A smart Joan would have answered J.B.'s original charge with something like the following.

Joan: "Oh, that is terrible! You're absolutely right, J.B. You're completely, totally, absolutely right. We can't afford this kind of screw-up. I'm terribly sorry. I don't know who's responsible or how it happened, but I'll sure as hell find out, J.B.!"

This is a good start. Note that smart Joan:

1. Totally agreed with J.B.

2. Shared and displayed his emotional response, thereby demonstrating

to J.B. that this outrageous emotional display was appropriate and nothing to be embarrassed about.

3. Apologized for the problem.

4. Didn't exactly admit that it was her fault.

5. Promised to get it fixed.

At that point, J.B. would have been almost totally defused and would begin to wind down. The typical boss would need a few additional minutes to cluck and sputter and release all the pent-up emotional energy that he or she thought would be necessary for a messy battle.

> *J.B.:* "Yes, well, yes. It is a very terrible problem. Yes, yes. And we can't afford this type of thing, no sir. This sort of thing makes us look bad, yes sir, very bad."

Joan is home free now. All she needs to do is flatter him a little more while he returns to normal.

> *Joan:* "Yes, you're absolutely right, J.B. We can't afford this type of thing. Our customers and our tradition of customer service are too important. I'll get right on this and find out what happened. I'll get back to you with a set of procedures to make sure this type of outrage doesn't happen ever again."

Now Joan is making some excellent moves. By promising to look into the situation and draw up some procedures, she is opening the door to an expansion of her control and authority. A not insignificant point is that she may even be able to shift the blame onto someone who deserves it (although this is a dangerous tactic; see Rule 21). J.B. is now totally defused and happy. He has only positive feelings to associate with Joan.

> *J.B.:* "Very good, very good. Yes, indeed. I'll look forward to seeing your recommendations."

If you do half as well as Joan the next time you're reprimanded, you'll be doing great. Once you have humbled yourself, get out of there as soon as possible. Do not brood about it afterward. You will have handled it as well as it could be handled. You have no control over a lot of important things. Sometimes the best you can do is to minimize the damage and future danger by reacting appropriately. If that's the case, just do it and move on; brooding about it will only cloud your magnificent rule-honed judgment for the next challenge.

Rule 53: Never say anything negative about anything to your boss.

Negative words are troublemakers in and of themselves. Words and expressions such as "no," "I don't like," "it isn't," "bad," or "can't" make people uncomfortable. The discomfort has two sources. The first is that negative words connote displeasure and/or disapproval with something. In the work environment, the disapproval is usually directed at some aspect of the organization's functioning or decision-making processes. Any attack, however small, on an organization irritates a lot of people. It threatens their illusion of security by demonstrating that the group bonds are not as strong as they fantasize and that the organization may not be as powerful and infallible as they'd like to think. Since bosses are more responsible than the workers for the state of the organization, they are more easily irritated by the implied attacks of negative words.

The second problem with negative words is that they are inherently threatening to the listener regardless of their implied attacks or content. When we were toddlers, our parents desperately tried to socialize us before every plant in the house was destroyed, before we ate everything under the kitchen sink, and before the cat's tail was permanently ruined. A large part of the socialization consisted of telling us "No!" and then pulling the leaves out of our mouths or extricating the cat from our sticky fingers. The verbal reprimand was accompanied by a stern look, perhaps a slap on the hand and our removal to another room. The emphasis was on "No!" and control of our behaviors. The result, now that we're grown up, is that we have ingrained emotional responses to negative words, particularly if they're directed at some action of ours. The implication of control tends to make us defensive and angry. It's a low-key response, buried by years of adult experience, but it's there. Avoid generating this negative emotional reaction as much as you can with your boss. The danger is that if you make enough negative comments, the low-grade emotional response of those who hear them will cause them to view you as a negative person. You'll seem too parental and controlling as if you're both passing judgment on them and trying to restrict their freedom of choice. This will occur because they will associate the discomfort they experience with your presence. The validity of what you say will be irrelevant. You must therefore avoid negative, controlling words as much as possible. The following list presents some typical negative comments and alternatives that mean the same thing (if you're clever enough to carry them out) but won't awaken the boss's emotional response to parental negatives.

Typical: "J.B., Joan is the stupidest, most limited manager I've ever seen. We've got to get rid of her."

Safer alternative: "J.B., Joan is working like a horse, but I think we need to find more appropriate duties that will benefit the company and allow her to grow."

Typical: "This marketing plan is the biggest piece of garbage I've ever seen."

Safer alternative: "This marketing plan has some great points. I think a little rework will make them shine even more."

Typical: "J.B., I tried to work up a proposal along the lines that you suggest, but I couldn't finish it. I just don't think the approach is right."

Safer alternative: "J.B., here's the proposal you wanted. It looks great! While I was working on it, I added a few bells and whistles I think will help. I'm sure you'll like it."

Of course, a certain number of negative comments have to be made. If you tried to avoid them all, your presentation would sound too stilted, too artificial, and fake. You can diminish the effect of necessary negatives by consistently presenting a positive, enthusiastic persona at all other times. No matter what happens, no matter how bad, you must always be enthusiastic. Even if your boss was personally responsible for the biggest two-year loss in the company's history, he or she will believe any flattery you dish out. If the boss tells you that the company just fell behind its arch rival in annual sales, you say, "Well, we're just going to have to go out there and blow them out of their socks next year!" If the boss tells you that you're going to have to lay off half of your department, you gush, "No sweat, Chief. This will give us a chance to clean house and get this place shaped up for the big push that's coming." You get the point. Be a beacon of enthusiasm, and it will light your way. What you may privately view as a healthy realism or properly somber emotional response will not be perceived that way. Remember, nobody can see inside your thoughts to tell what you are really thinking. To be safe, you must show them something that cannot possibly be misinterpreted. Cloying and constant enthusiasm is one of those things.

Rule 54: Always complete your responsibilities for your boss before any other duties.

Keeping your immediate boss happy and well managed is a large part of the business success challenge in most organizations. A big part of this effort involves showing the boss that you are dedicated and loyal.

This will cause the boss to be more relaxed and at ease when you're around. Getting the boss's work done first is one sure way to demonstrate your healthy attitude. Make sure the boss knows that this is your top priority, especially if you have duties for other people. Comments such as "Ms. Jacobs, I know you didn't have to have this report until Wednesday, but I have that special study to put together for the executive committee, and I wanted to tackle yours while I was still fresh" are good.

Naive and ignorant people don't think that their bosses have to be their number one priority. They think that if they can just get a little attention from the top, it will count more than their boss's favor and maybe even short-circuit the amount of work they'll have to do in order to get recognized. But to the folks higher up in the organization, you're only a piece of cheap metal furniture. They don't think about furniture very often, and when they do think about it, they think about leather and suede and fine woods, not the thin tin material your career is made of. Your boss holds the strings, and that's not going to change. Even if you impress someone higher up in the organization once in a while, your boss has the influence that will make or break you. Keep the boss happy first.

Rule 55: Never present your boss with an opportunity to unequivocally say yes or no.

Don't present ultimatums. Bosses have an almost religious attachment for simple yes or no decisions. Even though most bosses are fairly limited, many can handle a two-choice problem if given enough time. Since they are generally sitting on all sorts of complex decisions that they can't handle and that are generating a lot of guilt, they will leap at the chance to make a decision if it appears simple enough. Such action will demonstrate their "macho" business sense. You can't afford to have any of your programs hang on the random firing of a few neurons. Don't create such opportunities for problems by presenting clear yes or no decisions. It's far safer to move in small gradients over time, always assuming approval for the next small step but never asking outright for a yes or no answer. Once you have accumulated a history of small concessions on a project, you will then be in a position to ask for the last little bit. The boss will appreciate the opportunity to make the decision, and you'll get your program through.

> *Fred:* "Well, Priscilla, I've begun to implement the changes you recommended for reorganizing the Contracts department. I've prepared the promotion forms and the new job description for Johnson. I'll just leave it here for your review and signature."

Fred is learning. The boss would have to actually process some data—do some work—in order to shoot down the project. Since she's being flattered by the increasingly skillful Fred, Priscilla would have no reason to want to say no. Note that Fred also avoided the use of any negative expressions such as "*If* you want to approve it," "I fixed *the problem*," or "*I hope* you like it this time." Fred handled it beautifully. You can, too.

Rule 56: Always make sure that you receive all of the attention you need.

Don't let your emotional needs at a particular moment influence your decision about whether you should try to get the boss to notice you. Remember, a low positive profile is your strategy. If you are in a building phase and need to get the boss properly positioned, you may have to campaign carefully and subtly for as much notice as you can get. If you've been having some problems with the boss lately (probably because you thought you were experienced enough to know when to break the rules and go for the big play), you don't need the boss to know that you were just selected Jaycee of the month for all the time you give the community. Your boss may make some unpleasant assumptions about why you didn't have time to do a better job for him or her. In that case, you might want to reconsider sending the announcement of the award to your organization's newsletter. You should beat your own drum only when the boss is in the mood for your brand of drum music and you have a worthwhile tune to play.

Rule 57: Always praise your boss whenever possible, and always share the credit when you are praised for your work.

Many workers foolishly assume that if they share the credit for a recognized achievement, they are diminishing their stature within the hierarchy of the organization. This is an ignorant, short-sighted, and totally incorrect assumption. By publicly acknowledging that others have contributed to your success, you show yourself to be a team player, a company person, and a well-balanced, mature individual. On top of that, nobody thinks that you did any less work or that you made less of a contribution because you worked with others. As a matter of fact, your acknowledgments of others' help actually make your part look bigger because you get to talk about it more, more people hear about it, the others who share the credit get to talk about it, and you are seen more as a manager of a big effort than a solitary worker. Such press also serves to reinforce your image as someone who can work on tough problems as part of a complex team. This is a big asset in the eyes of the executives. So you come out looking even better when you share the credit. The advantages of doing this with bosses and superiors are even greater.

When you don't share the credit with your boss, you risk a lot more than missing out on the above advantages; you could also be getting your boss upset. It's part of the unspoken law of business that everybody makes the organization and their boss look good. That's just the way it is because of group and organizational dynamics. When you don't play the game, everybody knows it. Your boss realizes that you aren't a team player (the kiss of death if you want to move up to a more highly paid team), and your coworkers realize that you aren't supporting your work group so they won't help you out when you need it. There just isn't any way you can win if you try to hog the credit. Spread it around liberally; you'll look ten times better, and everybody will sing your praises as a real work horse, team player, and astute businessperson.

You can't afford to wait for opportunities to praise your boss; you won't get enough opportunities in most organizations if you just sit and wait. So take advantage of every chance to mention your boss's sterling qualities, even if he or she doesn't have any. The word will get back to the boss in a very short time. You will be seen as a true company person and team player. Consider the following exchange.

Jeff: "Hi, June. How's it going?"

June: "Great. How are you?"

Jeff: "Could be better. Pete messed up on his part of the annual plan, and now we all have to come in and work this weekend to run the projections over again. He's so disorganized!"

June: "That's too bad. I guess I'm lucky to report to Ms. Jacobs. She's so organized and methodical that no detail ever gets by her. She had her plan finalized three weeks ago."

Here June lays it on so thick that it's probably even making her sick; she's taking advantage of every opportunity to praise Ms. Jacobs. The trade-off is that her career will be very healthy. June's response makes Jeff a little frustrated. He wanted to engage in a little mutual grousing, but June wouldn't play. Not only did she not play, but she went further and praised her boss, thus making Jeff feel a little defensive. So Jeff tries once more to get June to engage in a little mutual grousing about their bosses.

Jeff: "Well, if she had it done three weeks ago, she must not have much to do!"

June: "Oh, no. She's always working on a lot of important projects. She routinely puts in twelve-hour days and comes in on the weekends.

Jeff now realizes that June will not rise to the bait. He'll avoid her the next time he wants to grouse. Not only will June benefit from Jeff's avoidance of her in general, but she'll look even better to Ms. Jacobs if her comments get back to her boss. And both Ms. Jacobs and June will benefit from the positive PR directed to their department in general, especially if others in the department are equally as crafty as June. Note that June did not allow herself to be constrained by considerations of actual facts. In reality, Ms. Jacobs hasn't worked a Saturday in five years, and she'd get lost if she attempted to find her way out of the parking lot in the dark. Learn from June's example. If you limit your praise of your boss to only justly deserved kudos, you won't be able to get in enough to do anyone any good.

Of course, if your boss is a recognized idiot, you must not pour it on too thick, or else you'll appear just as stupid. In that case, a little restrained praise will be recognized for what it really is: smart, polite courtesy from an astute person who knows what the organization wants. A lot of people are not mature enough to recognize that work is not the place to work out personal frustrations. These people refuse to generate any praise about their boss because they're trying to get even for real or imagined slights at the hands of the organization or the boss. These people are only worsening their fates. You can't dump on the boss and win. Not praising the boss is equivalent to dumping on the boss. Don't risk it; pour it on whenever you can.

Rule 58: Always use your boss's insecurities and fetishes to bolster your own programs and projects.

All bosses have a variety of pet insecurities, hot buttons, and fears.

Some constantly harp about worker productivity, some always want to see the bottom line, and others can't deal with anything unless it's marketing-oriented. Others are forever worrying about how busy everyone looks when upper management comes by, and some are addicted to detailed written reports and endless project meetings. Use these concerns and fetishes to your own advantage. If the boss is on the marketing kick, sprinkle your conversations with "strategic marketing plan" and "market penetration." If the boss has been reading about Japanese management techniques, mention zero inventory and Ouchi now and then. Your goal is to show the boss that you are worried about and dedicated to the same things he or she is. This will reduce the boss's anxiety about whether his or her programs are on target. The boss will then realize that you are an astute and perceptive person; after all, you're acting just like he or she acts. Notice how Mike, a compensation analyst in Personnel, plays on the personal computer fetish of Ms. Wilson, the Compensation/ Benefits manager. Ms. Wilson just recently became gung ho for computers when J.B. announced his intention to become more "systems-oriented." As happens to many persons who become exposed to computers for the first time, Ms. Wilson has gone totally overboard. She spends every free minute at the console, learning all sorts of things that have no possible use for her real job responsibilities. Mike knows a little about computers but is principally interested in installing a new performance appraisal system. Over the past two years, he hasn't had much luck in persuading Ms. Wilson to replace the antiquated one they have. Note how he uses her computer fetish to move her into agreement.

Mike: "Good morning, Rebecca. Hey, that looks like Orchestra 6-3-1 there. I didn't realize you were so advanced in your programming."

Ms. Wilson: "Yes, Mike. It's really impressive. Once I attend a few more classes, go to a few more three-day seminars, put in another couple of weeks here on the terminal, read a few more books, and spend some time with Johnson in Systems, I think I'll know enough to start putting together a computerized compensation report that'll only take an hour to produce instead of the three hours it now takes one of the clerks every month. J.B. will really be impressed."

Mike: "That's really great. You know, that program can also do a lot of data management work as well. I was thinking that we could use its capabilities and those of another software package or two to reconfigure our performance appraisal system so that we can keep the records on the computer. What do you think?"

Mike knows full well that it doesn't make any difference whether the records are kept in a computer or in a file cabinet. But he also knows that Ms. Wilson is hot for computers and that any project that uses a computer for any purpose at all will go through the approval cycle rapidly.

Ms. Wilson: "Sounds great. I'm glad to see that you appreciate the inherent value of computerization to a modern Personnel department. I'll tell J.B. about the new performance appraisal system that we're working on. He'll love it."

Mike: "Rebecca, I really appreciate the support. I'll put together a preliminary outline that will describe the new front-end reports that'll provide the input to the computer. I'll show it to you in a week or so, OK?"

Ms. Wilson: "Great. I can't wait to get started on it with you."

Simply by playing on Ms. Wilson's computer fetish, Mike has been able to win approval to do the very same thing he'd been trying to push for two years. It doesn't make any difference that the wisdom or justification for a new performance appraisal system should be made on the basis of other factors; it's a computer issue now, and heaven help the poor fool who tries to stop it on rational grounds. Mike did a good job of waiting until management's interests presented an appropriate vehicle for selling his programs. You can easily do the same thing if you pay attention to the latest fad that management is hot for. There are so many that you should have no problem finding one that can provide protective cover for your programs and, at the same time, help demonstrate that you're enthusiastically on board the organization bandwagon. A big part of these types of efforts is nothing more than jargon, particularly if you're just trying to impress the boss rather than sell an idea. They're so easy to use that it's a crime if you don't.

Rule 59: Never be open and candid with your boss.

Many times it will be in your best interests to appear to be open and candid with the boss. That's OK as long as you are not actually being open and candid. You can never come out ahead if you level with the boss. If the boss says something like "Mary, I want you to tell me what you really think of the way I'm running the office," the hairs on the back of your neck should stand straight up; you are in mortal danger. Remember, executives only want to hear what they know and what they like (Rule 14). Chances are that the boss will not like the truth. Even if the boss would like the truth, you can't risk it because you can never be sure. In such situations, you must remain cool and calm and avoid emotional responses. Many people react emotionally to the boss's apparent candor because they think they are getting closer to the boss. Maybe they are, but it's no safer than getting closer to a cranky cobra. Handle your response carefully. A proper, safe reply to the above question from J.B. would be something along the lines of "Well, J.B., you're doing as much with the resources that anyone could expect." If the boss presses for more, don't react emotionally and relax your defenses; the fangs are inches from your next promotion's jugular. Stay positive and general. If you absolutely have to provide negative information in order to help the boss engage in guilt-reducing self-flagellation, keep it to positive negatives, such as:

"Well, J.B., you may not realize it, but not everybody is as dedicated as you are. What seems like a normal work load to you is too much for some of our people. When they can't handle it, they get frustrated, and they start complaining and causing trouble. I say that if they can't shape up, they should ship out."

In the above example, the boss is told that he missed something only because of the white-hot heat of his surging creativity and work output. This type of response gives an acceptable amount of candid criticism. Almost any boss can handle that type of "criticism." Don't risk any more.

Rule 60: Always praise the quality of work that your people produce.

Never complain about what your employees do or don't do. What they do and don't do and what people say about them are direct reflections on you. You must always give the impression that your people are working their guts out for you and loving it. If you have a personnel problem, deal with it as much as you can without the boss. If your organization is like most others, you'll be expected to manage "on your own," "independently," and "like a tiger," but you'll have to get endless approvals to do anything to the status of an employee. If this is the case, do all of your homework and get the advance work done (written reprimands, and so on) before you finally have to tell your boss about it. You'll then have the documentation complete and the employee ready to terminate. This approach shortens the amount of time in which you are visible with the problem employee.

Do the same with all of your difficulties. If you go to the boss with a problem the minute you see it, you are looking for trouble. And you'll find it repeatedly. Every time you see the boss, he or she is going to ask how it's going, whether it's any better, and so on. Worse yet, the boss may decide how you should handle it. All of a sudden, your one little problem is going to be the focus of most of the attention you get from your boss. You don't need the boss making that type of association. When it is necessary to let the boss know about a problem, keep it short and positive so that the problem will seem like a minor detail.

> *Problem:* One of your employees has consistently disobeyed your orders regarding approvals for checks. As a result, the company has lost $15,000 that it can't track.

> *You say:* "Yes, sir. Everything is great, Mr. Preston. We've got a minor ledger error of $15,000 that we're on top of, but it's no problem. Incidentally, Jeff doesn't seem like he's got the stuff to make it to the next level of management. If we're trying to build for the future, we may have to do the tough thing and consider bringing in someone with more future potential."

Note that your handling included several key points. You downplayed the problem Jeff created, downplayed his inherent defect to something that's not a problem now, reinforced your boss's perception that you believe the organization has a future, and gave the boss an opportunity to make an easy decision because he'll leap at the chance to be "tough."

If you go on and on about your woes, it will serve only to make the problem bigger and your management skills smaller. At all other times, spread around lots of praise for your people. Present a cheery, "they couldn't be a better group" attitude. Don't complain about anything they do to anyone. If there's a problem, fix it, and keep as quiet about it as you can. You will be viewed as a good manager, and your employees will eventually hear about it and respect you for making them look good.

Rule 61: Never discuss unsolicited information with your boss.

Simply keeping away from the boss (Rule 46) is not enough. You must also limit the amount of unsolicited information you give to the boss. Providing unsolicited or excessive data is just as bad and sometimes more damaging than mere proximity. Most bosses can't or won't make decisions as a result of incompetence or anxiety. When you present more information than they ask for, you're placing a burden on them. One of two things will happen, both of which are bad for you. First, if they're feeling particularly guilty or anxious, they may impulsively make an on-the-spot decision. Such a decision will be purely an emotional release and will not involve the facts. The more likely response will be that they'll react to your input by doing something that will delay the need for anyone to make a decision. Most often, this delay takes the form of asking you to do more investigation, suggesting that you put together a proposal, or telling you to get a committee together to "take a look at it." You'll end up doing five times as much work just so the boss can delay having to make a decision. And when the boss eventually can't put it off any longer without being an obvious idiot, he or she will probably make the wrong one and ruin all of your efforts. In addition, your boss will be angry with you for having created an additional administrative burden (making him or her have to "manage" you as you do the decision-delaying work) as well as for having made him or her feel guilty. Many career losers look for ways to prolong encounters with the boss, thinking that such contact is good. For example, note how Betty, the manager of Quality Assurance at ABC Company, blows it in a meeting with Ms. Jacobs, to whom she reports. Betty is new to the company and a little insecure. She knows nothing about the rules. She's been thinking about putting in a quality circles program in her department, something that's totally within her scope of authority. However, she wants to impress Ms. Jacobs as well as prolong the "cozy with the boss" feelings she's enjoying during their meeting.

   Ms. Jacobs: "Well, Betty, I guess that's about it until our regular staff meeting next week."

Betty should have taken the hint and gotten out fast. But she blurts out the big news.

   Betty: "Oh, I forgot to mention it, but I'm thinking of setting up a quality circles program in the second shift. I've read a lot about them, and I think we've got just the right kind of operation that'd fit with the concept. What do you think?"

Asking the boss "What do you think?" about an unsolicited topic is more dangerous than dangling your bloody career in a pool of starving corporate MBAs. In this sorry case, Betty is unaware that J.B. talked about quality circles in his last executive staff meeting. It seems that J.B. ran into an old friend of his who used them in the company that his dad left him. J.B. decided on the spot that ABC Company should have quality circles, too. Ms. Jacobs correctly sees Betty's suggestion as a way to get in good with J.B. by capitalizing on one of his latest fetishes.

> *Ms. Jacobs:* "That sounds like a good idea, but I think we should do it with all shifts at once. And we'll offer to train group leaders for other departments in the company."
>
> *Betty:* "Well, that could be a problem. I wanted to start with the second shift because it'd be a small pilot program and I could train all the group leaders myself. The second shift would require only five group leaders. The first shift would require over forty-five group leaders. That's a lot of training time."
>
> *Ms. Jacobs:* "We don't have any choice. J.B. is hot for a QC program, and you're the expert on it. We'll just have to make the time. We can always do the training on Saturdays."

There go Betty's Saturdays as well as the control of the program. Note the "We don't have any choice." Seconds before, Ms. Jacobs wasn't even going to do anything but wait for one of her peers to take the lead. But Betty's suggestion got her rolling. By the time all the others in the company jump on the bandwagon, Betty will have no say whatsoever. All she'll end up doing is the work on Saturdays. Betty will also have the honored privilege of taking all the blame if things don't work out as planned.

In addition to keeping your meetings with your boss as informationally sparse as possible, the little information that you'll be forced to provide must never be based upon assumptions that you know what your boss is thinking about a particular topic or what his or her hidden motives might be. Such assumptions can get a good career into a lot of trouble in a very short time.

> *Ms. Baylor:* "Well, J.B., I've completed the arrangements for the retirement dinner for Mr. Paul."
>
> *J.B.:* "Good, good. Now, who do you have sitting with Mr. Paul, Mr. Noggins, and myself at the head table?"
>
> *Ms. Baylor:* "Mr. Preston, the controller, Mr. Jenkins, the Operations VP, and Ms. Jones."
>
> *J.B.:* "What is Ms. Jones doing up there with all the brass?"
>
> *Ms. Baylor:* "Well, I thought Mr. Paul would appreciate it. Everyone knows that Ms. Jones and Mr. Paul have been having an affair for the past three years."

I will spare the ugly details concerning Ms. Baylor's career progression from that point on; it wasn't quick, and it wasn't pretty. Suffice it to say that J.B. didn't know. In fact, Ms. Jones and J.B. were also involved. A more successful Ms. Baylor, recognizing that J.B. was a little alarmed, would have assumed nothing and would have answered something like the following.

> *More successful Ms. Baylor:* "Well, J.B., I thought it would be a good morale booster for the troops to see one of the gang from the Tax department up there with all of you. What do you think?"

This reply assumed nothing other than J.B.'s support for established organizational goals ("We're all in it together" and "We're all equal here"). The only safe course is to take nothing for granted. The only way you can do that with confidence is to offer as little information as possible.

Rule 62: Never go over your boss's head.

It is an ironclad rule of organizations that you don't go over your boss's head no matter what the reason. People who do are usually greeted with a response such as, "Well, Fred, all of the board members are shocked, of course, to hear this news about J.B., but we are disappointed that you felt it was necessary to come to us with this. Couldn't you have worked it out with J.B.?" Your career is dead at that organization. The brass now believes that you can't be trusted with anything. Of course, you can, but they don't think so. They actually have a sound reason for discouraging this sort of activity. If end running is allowed, it destroys the fabric of the reporting structure. Pretty soon, everybody is going straight to the top with everything.

One company was run by an ex-Army type who fostered this sort of activity all the time. It was doubly strange that an ex-military officer would condone such activities, but you don't get to the top in the service by acting that way. I hypothesized that he didn't really have any concept of how civilian businesses were run, having been in the service most of his adult life. He probably assumed that the business world just had to operate 180 degrees differently from the army. He was, of course, wrong; any differences between the two in terms of inefficiency and bureaucracy are only quantitative, not qualitative. He apparently felt that businesses are run without formal and informal authority structures and that executives can, without penalty, interfere in the activities of all levels of the organization. Under this martinet's reign, every single decision in the organization, including even individual merit pay raises for factory workers all around the country, had to get his signature. More damaging than the inefficiency caused by this type of micro-management meddling was his failure to create a responsive, committed management team. You don't build solid organizations without letting each level of management function somewhat independently. Any employee who didn't like your face on a particular day could simply call the head shed and spill his guts. Ten minutes later you'd get a ranting, raving phone call. The result was that everyone was afraid to do anything or make any decisions that might be second guessed by someone else. There was no innovation, no risk taking, no enthusiasm, no experimentation, and ultimately no real responsibility. No organization run in that manner can be successful over the long haul. Real workers can't tolerate that type of environment for very long. The dregs who stay are the milksops of the business world; they can march where you tell them, but they can't walk on their own. In today's business environment, an organization that doesn't foster experimentation and initiative won't be able to survive changes in its markets or technologies. The best way to crush everyone's spirit is to allow a lot of end running; everybody gets too scared to take a chance. So you can see that organizations have a good reason for dumping on end runners. Don't play this game; it will wreck you and your organization.

Rule 63: Do not call your boss's attention to unfavorable news about the boss or the department.

Remember Rule 16 about executives always being suspicious about everyone's motives? That's one reason for not coming to the boss with anything. Bad news is even more dangerous. If you walk in and attempt to diplomatically point out that Customer Billing is upset because the department can never communicate the customer's needs, the boss may start to think that you're one of those ''bean-counter lovers.'' And if the problem is the boss himself or herself, not the department as a whole, how is the boss going to react to a personal slur that you were kind enough to point out? You begin to get the picture. If the news is all that bad, the boss will get it through regular channels (let someone else ruin his or her career).

The one exception is when you have personally made a big mistake that is going to cause a lot of embarrassment when the word gets out or the consequences hit. In that case, admit the error as soon as possible.

If your boss has time to prepare a defense, the ultimate damage to all concerned will be reduced. If the information concerns another member of the department, just leave it alone completely. I've seen situations where the boss, when informed by employee A of something that employee B had said or done that caused the department trouble, immediately called in employee B. With both employees in the room, the boss then proceeded to try to find out what was happening. Needless to say, poor old employee A ended up being humiliated by employee B, who lied. Worse yet, employee B then spread the word that employee A could not be trusted because he would "run and blab everything to the boss." If a situation like this happens to you, just keep your mouth shut and ride out the storm. Your advance warning of bad news probably wouldn't save the department enough trouble to justify all the trouble it could cause you. There's less risk in getting your career a little wet with all the others when the departmental boat takes on water. If you are the solitary bearer of bad news, your career may get totally swamped all by itself, and nobody will be standing by to help you bail.

Rule 64: Never attempt to promote yourself at the expense of someone else who reports to your boss.

You must keep things in perspective. When you attempt to advance yourself at someone else's expense, you are doing so on the basis of a distorted view of reality: your narrow one. You are intimately aware of your own creativity, energy, and potential. Your boss, on the other hand, must worry about his or her own boss's perceptions. The whole world isn't standing by anxiously to see what you can do. Your boss likes to foster and be comforted by the belief that the entire department is pulling together to make him or her look good. Anything that disrupts that perception is not going to be welcomed. If you dump all over a competitor in your boss's department, you create a no-win situation. If the boss allows you to win, it means that someone else in the department must lose. Your boss doesn't want any losers and will not think kindly of the person who creates one; to your boss, it's a wash. Having one winner and one loser doesn't help. Worse still, if you let yourself be seen even slightly as a hatchet man (and in a department, it's hard to hide a power move), not only will you get the boss irritated, but you may also inspire the troops to make revenge efforts against you. And, believe me, they'll work harder at those than they would ever work at their jobs. If you play the game, follow the rules, and have patience, your efforts will be rewarded. The others will make mistakes and will fall behind you. You won't have to hurt them to come out ahead. Nobody will blame you for their failings. In fact, you will be viewed as a "rock," someone who can be depended on.

7

Rules for Supervising Your Employees

The typical boss who reads Chapter 6 will probably feel that he or she has been unfairly characterized as insensitive, incompetent, lazy, and technically unqualified. Let's face it, Chapter 6 doesn't paint a very flattering picture of the boss. Sometimes the truth hurts. If you're a boss and feel that you've been unjustly characterized, hold off on your judgment until you read this chapter. If you're following the rules presented in this chapter, you're one of the very few bosses out there who is doing what you're supposed to be doing: managing your people in an efficient, humane, creative, and cost-effective manner. If you're not following most of the rules in this chapter, you're a bad boss, plain and simple. If you are a bad boss, then your employees are probably thinking about you in the same light that Chapter 6 used to characterize all bosses. They think you're a total, vindictive, and disorganized buffoon. It's not too late to change, although it is very difficult. If you're still nurturing hopes of making it big, you don't have any choice; you're going to need the hard work of your employees to get there. If you don't manage them properly, you're stacking the odds against yourself.

If you're not a boss yet, this chapter is just as important. You'll have the incredible career advantage of learning how to manage your employees before you screw things up as badly as your present boss probably has done. As you read the rules in this chapter, just consider how much more motivated you'd be if your boss used the rules approach in dealing with you rather than his or her present system.

This is the longest chapter in the book because it's the most important. If you make it big in business, you're going to do so largely on the merits of those who work for you. No matter how gifted you are, you'll look like a real loser if your employees cause a lot of problems or don't get the work done correctly. You're going to have to ride to success on their backs; you'd better take the trouble to see that they don't come up lame or feel inclined to throw you. The proper management and motivation of other people in the unnatural environment of the workplace is the single greatest challenge in modern business. It's a challenge that most bosses don't meet.

Rule 65: Never forget that supervision is an active, daily process.

You can let a lot of things in business slide without getting caught. In most organizations, for instance, the preparation of the annual plan and budget is a big joke. Everyone waits until the last minute and then just jacks up last year's figures by 5 or 10 percent, pads as many extra slots into it as they think they can get away with, and hopes that nobody asks any detailed questions. I've seen this happen in three-person companies and in Fortune 20 conglomerates. Most of the time, everybody gets away with it. Supervision of employees is another story. Whether or not your organization values its people as a real asset, things are going to be a lot more difficult for you personally if you wait for supervisory problems to appear before you work on them.

Your people are not in a state of limbo when you aren't working directly with them or thinking about them. Every day they come to work, worry about their own problems, make value judgments about what you and the organization want them to do, and attempt to play the game according to their perceptions of the rules. Each one of them does these things at a different speed and with a different degree of skill. In order to keep everything moving in a reasonable fashion, you must constantly be observing, counseling, measuring, adjusting, praising, scolding, and showing the flag, showing them that "we're all in this together." If you're not involved in a significant manner on a day-to-day basis, you'll be powerless to avert disaster. Good supervision is much like launching a radio-controlled missile: You set the original course, launch it, monitor it, and make minor corrections if things get a little off course. Bad managers act as if good supervision were analogous to firing a mortar: They just aim it, fire, and pray. If you want to be a success at work, you'd better manage your employees on a daily basis so they don't stray too far from the course you've charted for your success.

Rule 66: Never assume that your employees are as dedicated as you are.

If you make this assumption, you will be repeatedly and sorely disappointed. People work for many reasons, usually the least of which is a careful and well-thought-out concern for their career development. You would be lucky beyond reason if each of your employees were to read this book and follow the rules. In that case, they would be carefully attending to your sensitivities, not bothering you about their petty emotional states and problems, and looking out for their careers (which would help yours). You'll get no such luck. Instead, most of them will merely consider the workplace as another locale in which to act out the ongoing soap opera of their personal lives. Most of the time, they'll be governed by urges that are directly contrary to their own best career interests but will serve their short-term emotional needs. Faced with this sorry state of affairs, you would be foolish to assume that your employees are as dedicated to doing a good job and furthering their careers as you are. Until each of them proves the contrary, don't rely on them to carry through independently on difficult assignments.

In addition to the hordes of people who aren't motivated to work as hard as you, there are many who aren't motivated to work at all. And you're going to find that there's not much, outside of firing them, that you can do about it, at least not by techniques that are legal. You have relatively little control over people's lives at work. The fact is that many workers don't work for pride and self-satisfaction. Many other workers don't perceive that they must work hard just for money. After all, they see hosts of government workers who do what they perceive as little for their pay, they see highly paid executives with incredible fringes and luxuries who are obviously not about to keel over with fatigue, and they know they can find another job similar to their present one if anyone rides them enough. And not a few workers just don't have to work if they don't want to. Their spouses make enough to live on, and they are just working for the extras such as quarterly trips to Mexico or Hawaii, jewelry, or a new car every year. With workers like these, you are going to find that you are severely limited in motivating them to increased productivity. Threats and reprimands aren't effective for motivating anyone for more than a short time. Behavior modification programs get a lot of attention but aren't generally effective. A brief description of one behavior modification program will demonstrate just how far some poorly informed managers will go in futile attempts to motivate the unmotivatable.

The very expensive behavior modification program was bought by a Los Angeles area hospital from a well-known firm that specializes in these types of programs. Elaborate reporting and point reward systems were devised for every supervisor and manager. For some misguided reason, the program was not introduced to the rank and file, a group in which it may have had at least a chance of success. Each manager had to spend at least four hours per week compiling data and drawing graphs. The department managers then had to attend another two hours of individual meetings each week with a person who was hired on a full-time basis to do nothing but collect all the graphs and charts. If an employee or department got enough points, they could order merchandise from a catalog that had the smiling face of the administrator on the inside front cover.

The program failed miserably for several all too common reasons. First of all, most of the employees did not live at or near the poverty line. To these employees, the perceived value of a new pair of earrings or a toaster wasn't great enough to lead to any changes in their behavior. You're dealing with people who were going to Club Med every three months. Secondly, the overall performance of the facility was abysmal in terms of profits, morale, and management skills. You can't expect any type of motivation system to work when it is superimposed on a rotten framework. People in the facility were routinely taking two and three days off per week (unreported and with pay, of course). Would they work harder (when they were there) for a new blender? I doubt it. A third reason why it failed was that everyone was permitted to design his or her own point reward system. They cleverly set up systems with which they could appear to be working hard (accumulating massive point totals) while they were actually doing less than before the program started (because they now had to devote some of their limited in-facility time to drawing graphs and charts). Once things have been allowed to get that bad, you'd have to start chopping and replacing before you could rebuild. If the organization doesn't think it has a serious problem, you'd better not try to do any chopping at all. Such situations are the ones that will demand the best of your talents as a supervisor, getting the most out of a terrible mess while looking good and maintaining a positive low profile.

Rule 67: Never assume that all employees are equally skilled or intelligent.

Organizations and executives boast that their employees are a highly skilled and intelligent group of professionals. If such assertions were true, you'd have to ask yourself, "Where do all the stupid and incompetent people drive off to each morning?" The answer, of course, is that they drive to their jobs, some of them to work for your organization. Do not put your career on the line by making careless assumptions about the abilities or skills of employees simply because they already hold a job or because they look the part. I was once introduced to a young man who had just joined the organization from a top school with an MBA. He had been hired on the basis of his degree, school, and personal appearance. He was tall, blond, and good-looking, with an athletic physique and a ready smile. It was thought that he would win over many accounts on appearance alone. Unfortunately, he was an idiot who couldn't even use the phone properly. This is not a particularly extreme case. In every organization, there are many individuals who appear to be capable but are not. They develop artful ways to fill their time and appear busy. They are also dangerous to your career. Identify these people, and get rid of them as soon as it is safe to do so. If you can't get rid of them without creating potentially serious visibility problems, watch them very carefully. Don't assign critical tasks to them, and don't expect them to follow through on anything. Don't be taken in by appearances, and do not make dangerous assumptions.

Rule 68: Communicate to your employees that it is in their own best interest to talk positively about the department, their colleagues, and you.

This is critical. If you have to resort to threats (made privately on an individual basis so that there are no witnesses), do it. One bad word about your department or yourself from one of your people is worse than fifty from outsiders. The best way to instill these positive values is through your own example. By carefully following the rules, you will automatically provide the proper role model. It will take time for them to observe your actions and come into line, but it will work. It will work even if you've been breaking all of the rules up until today and suddenly change when you go to work tomorrow. If you have stubborn cases or slow learners, conduct a private attitude adjustment conference as often as necessary with each of them. Point out your concerns, and tell them specifically what behaviors you expect from them. In an atmosphere where everyone is saying only positive things or nothing at all, all of the department members will eventually come to change their own attitudes. The perception of outsiders about your department will improve after only a few weeks of uniformly positive output from your own people. Stay hard on this rule; it's critical. If someone can't be brought into line, begin to take steps to ease them out. Write them up formally every chance you get. (It isn't too hard because these people are usually wasting so much time being bitter that they can't get their jobs done.) If they haven't shaped up by the time you're ready to take action, fire them or move them to low-visibility positions. It's your career or theirs.

Rule 69: Fight for your deserving employees at every safe opportunity.

Your employees must be led to believe that you are their advocate to management and the protector of their rights. They must believe that you will defend them from unjustified and unsupported abuse from the organization. They must also believe that they stand to gain more by virtue of working for you rather than someone else. The only way to make them believe this is to actually do it. Unless you are a true superstar, you will not be able to do all the work yourself, and it would be foolish to try; you've got better things than the technical work to do with your time. The only way you can ensure that you have enough time and energy to attend to your career interests is to develop a dedicated group of employees who will watch out for your interests while pumping out the work. In order for you to get the most out of them in the most effective manner, they must believe that you take good care of them. Always be willing to ''go to the mat'' for each of them.

For example, let's say that one of your employees has complained that he has the same duties and responsibilities as a worker in another department but has a less prestigious job title and gets slightly less money. It would be easy to let this one pass and simply blame it on Personnel or ''the system.'' If there are not serious risks involved, go ahead and have a little fun, and help out your employee at the same time. The advantage (aside from pure enjoyment) that derives from taking on Personnel for one of your people is that it looks a lot harder than it is. It'll take forever because of all of the Personnel department's innate inefficiencies. You'll have to attend countless meetings, take a lot of phone calls, and review an endless series of revised job descriptions. After the preliminaries, Personnel will then have to "factor" the job description. This process can be depended upon to occupy most Personnel analysts for one to three weeks. By the time you have finished getting the pay increase and new job title, the employee will think that you have won a momentous and tortuous victory. He will spread the tale of your incredible feat and compassion to everyone he knows. Everybody will think you're a great boss, just what you want them to think. That's not bad for a total investment of about thirty minutes of your time over six to eight weeks, is it?

Of course, you must never recklessly look for these types of challenges. Use them only to further your own rule following. There may be cases where you cannot afford the exposure such a conflict would require. If that's the case, avoid the challenge and maintain the low profile you will have come to love. Many otherwise successful managers hurt their careers by engaging in interdepartmental battles out of boredom. Remember, you are not at work to enjoy yourself or even to do the work; you're there to be a success. If it was fun getting to the top, everybody would be a success.

One last word: Never ever fight a battle for an employee who doesn't deserve it. You never want to demonstrate that you'll do anything for someone who doesn't vigorously support you and your department at all times and in all areas.

Rule 70: Never demean any of your employees to anyone for any reason.

The demeaning comment can be very subtle, such as "You know how Bob gets when we get in a proposal meeting," or incredibly dangerous, as in "I've really had it with John's mouthing off in the staff meetings." No matter how justified you are, it will get back to someone who will perceive it improperly. At the very best, you will be seen as a not so charitable person. At the worst, your own people will see the inconsistency between your "let's all pull together" presentation and your back-biting actions. If your unkind comments are about the quality of the work itself, you're digging your own grave. After all, these people work for you, don't they? It's your job to see that they perform or get out. Talking about it doesn't help. If you're not going to do anything to fix the problem, keep quiet about it.

You can't win by dumping on your people in any manner, even in jest. Despite the obvious danger, a lot of people do it, probably out of their frustration with the particular employee. It's understandable but dangerous. Your jest also serves to lower your own perceived status. Your employees and yourself are perceived by everybody else as members of one group. Anything that lowers the status of one of the group's members also serves to lower the status of all members of the group. If you've got a problem employee, relieve the frustration by spending some extra time with that employee. Try to change either the employee's problem or your perception of it. If that doesn't work, spend the time by building a case for getting rid of the problem. But don't make it bigger by grousing to your boss, your peers, or anyone else.

Rule 71: Always maintain a high degree of visibility among your employees.

This accomplishes several important goals. Your employees will work better when they know you are likely to show up. Those who work for your direct approval will be looking forward to the opportunity to get a "well done" from the boss. Those who are inclined to work at less than white-hot heat will not want to be caught loafing. Even more important is the group cohesiveness you'll generate by sharing some informal, non-meeting time with your employees. A supervisor who neglects this rule runs the risk of actually becoming an "outsider" to his or her own people. This happens to a lot of otherwise good managers every day. They can't find the time from what they consider to be the more important tasks in order to circulate among their own employees. In a short time, the manager becomes one of "them" (management in general) and is not considered part of the group. Once your employees develop this attitude, they'll be less concerned about how both you and the department look to the rest of the organization. If they consider you an outsider, there will be less group cohesion and less positive PR spread around by the group. You don't want your employees to think of you as "one of the boys or girls," but you do want them to perceive you as the group leader in substance as well as title. They won't do this unless you spend some meaningful time in group interactions.

A very important side benefit of this visibility will be the positive impression such interactions will give to your superiors. They like nothing better than to see one of their people out there in the trenches.

Be careful, though, not to allow your interactions to become fraternal or social. And do not attempt to foster this group cohesion among employees who report more than two levels beneath you. It can't work. Chances are that you're not familiar with their group's socioeconomic customs, beliefs, and expectations. And you probably don't know enough about the work they do to make any intelligent comments about it. They know all of these things, and they'll be wondering what your problem is. Even under the best of circumstances, you would most likely be highly suspect to the uneasy workers. And your supervisors would consider it inappropriate for you to be meddling with their people and end running them. Let the supervisors of your lower-level employees worry about maintaining direct and interactive contact with their people. Your task is to concentrate on doing the same with the people who report directly to you.

Rule 72: Do not socialize with your employees.

The less your employees know about you personally, the better off you will be. Social situations invariably include rituals that require some personal disclosures. You don't need the trouble this can bring. Once employees begin to think that they know you, they will begin to do what everyone does with their friends: They will get more informal. This will lead to rash assumptions on their part about what you want, laxity in their work habits (out of reduced fear), and a general loss of the cold formality in which your image as a professional will grow. Let's face it, once they find out that you held the campus record for nude streaking through the coed dormitories, or that your spouse bosses you around shamelessly at home, you're not going to be viewed with the same awe and respect that they held on the first day they worked for you.

At the same time, you cannot appear to be antisocial or unfriendly, particularly at official company functions. Attendance at such functions is critical to your success. But do it right. Smile a lot, circulate through the crowd, make sure everyone sees that you're there, and then leave as soon as you can. Don't have more than one drink, don't dance with the most attractive member of the opposite sex that you can find, and don't use your scintillating wit to become the center of attention for the group in Purchasing. Do the same thing during your more typical day-to-day activities. Smile a lot, appear pleasant and outgoing, have a kind or interesting word for some of your employees, but don't say anything of much substance and keep the interactions short and harmless. Always leave the impression that you'd love to stay and talk but you can't because you're busy and pressed for time.

Rule 73: Never confide in your employees.

Never make the mistake of thinking that you can confide something personal to one of your employees and have it stay a secret. It can't happen. Everyone likes to know something special about the boss. Unfortunately, everyone also wants everyone else to know that he or she is the only one who knows it. It makes people feel special. The only way to prove it is to tell. Sooner or later, your little secret will be out. Ms. Jacobs overlooked this rule two years ago, and she's still paying for it. In late November, she walked into her office and met Hallie, a management trainee, who had just dropped off a report.

Hallie: "Oh, hi, Priscilla. Been Christmas shopping?"

Ms. Jacobs: "Yes, it's really a mob scene out there. The crowd over at Dorfman's was incredible. But it was worth it; they had some great buys."

Hallie: "Yeah, I like to shop at Dorfman's, too. I just bought some lingerie there last week. Their stuff is expensive, but it's a great buy if it's on sale. What did you get today?"

This is where Ms. Jacobs blew it. She'd had a nice lunch and a glass of wine, was suffused with the Christmas spirit, and was pleased to have found some real buys. Ms. Jacobs was feeling relaxed and friendly. In that condition, her resistance to Hallie's "getting close to the boss" maneuvers was low. As a result, Ms. Jacobs let out a delicious little secret.

Ms. Jacobs: "Well, Hallie, don't tell anyone, but my husband has this thing about black lace panties. So I wear them on special occasions, if you know what I mean."

Hallie (speaking): "I think that's cute."

(thinking): "And so will the crew at the coffee machine. Wait until I tell everyone that Ms. Jacobs's gorilla of a husband likes black lace panties!"

Ms. Jacobs: "Well, I also bought...."

Three weeks later at the Christmas party, the department staff exchanged gifts. Ms. Jacobs was surprised and shocked to receive a pair of black lace panties from Lloyd, who had drawn her name the week before. The card read, "Say hi to hubby for us." Even after two years, everyone who joins the company hears the story in clinical detail. You can bet that everyone's first thought when they see Ms. Jacobs is to wonder if she's wearing them now. That's just what Ms. Jacobs needed to help develop her aura of professionalism, especially among the mostly male high-level executives. Of course, Hallie paid for her loose lips when Ms. Jacobs turfed her some months later. Unfortunately, the damage was done. Ms. Jacobs had been shocked and outraged that her secret got out, but she hurt herself. There are no secrets. You may as well assume that anything you tell to one employee will automatically appear in the memories of the others, with the only lag being the time it takes them to get from you to anyone else in the department with ears.

Rule 74: Conduct yourself as if you were the company.

You may not feel very significant sometimes, especially when you've just been reprimanded by your version of J.B. or Ms. Jacobs and you're up to your fraternity pin in dirty work. But in the eyes of your employees, you are the company. When they talk about the place where they work, they most often will talk about their boss. You hold a very significant position in their lives. If you make enough small mistakes in how you handle them, they will like nothing better than to spend hours talking with glee about your deficiencies to anyone who will listen. In that kind of environment, almost anything you do will be twisted until it looks like a mistake. You don't need that kind of press.

A very dangerous aspect of their view of you as the company is that you are going to be held responsible for a lot of things the organization does to them. If one of their friends in another department gets fired, your employees are going to be upset and angry at the organization. Part of that anger will be directed at you because you're seen as part of the organization's decision-making apparatus. You know that you've got relatively little of the power or influence they perceive, but they don't, and they wouldn't believe it even if you were foolish enough to admit it. You've got to work hard to build up working—not personal— relationships with your people so that they will know that you are not "like the organization" when something bad happens and/or they feel they've been cheated. You must help them to perceive that you are more fair, more protective of them, and more likely than other managers to help them get somewhere. In that way, you'll be able to dissociate yourself from the effect of the organization's many thoughtless and ruthless maneuvers. At the same time, you'll automatically be associated with everything good that the organization does (such as new benefits or an across-the-board pay raise) because they'll still perceive that you're part of management. More importantly, they'll want to believe nice things about you.

Rule 75: Never display an arrogant or condescending manner with your employees.

It has been hypothesized that prolonged exposure to supple leathers, private covered parking, plush carpets, fine woods, low work pressure, and no arguments leads to the development of a unique corporate psychosis. When overcome with this malady, the executive acts in a condescending and arrogant manner to people who do not share the delusion—those whose exposure is limited to smaller offices with linoleum floors, incredible work pressures, and parking lots a mile from the building. Only the psychosis hypothesis can account for the fact that intelligent adults can so often overlook the effects that arrogant behavior has on other people. We all know how we react when someone sneers, "Well, just what makes you think you have the answer?" or if someone ignores us when we say hello. Yet a lot of senior-level executives have come to conclude that an arrogant and superior demeanor is the appropriate robe of office. They are letting their personal emotional needs dictate their behavior. They are asking for big trouble. You can act slightly aloof and distant without being arrogant and condescending. The employees may not think you're the friendliest person in the world, but that's OK. At least they won't generate any negative press about you. They expect a manager to be slightly distant, aloof, and preoccupied. In fact, they may feel you're not a good manager if you're not a little cool to them. (It makes contact with you seem more special.) The key to appearing somewhat cool, and thus professional, is courtesy. Courtesy and a smile will be interpreted as showing that you're a nice person. The short length of your encounters and your brisk manner will speak for your professionalism.

Rule 76: Do not be candid with employees about any doubts you may have about the organization.

Your success depends upon a smooth, unblemished facade of overwhelming enthusiasm and optimism about the company from your employees and yourself. The slightest imperfection in such a smooth surface will attract a lot of attention. The revelation on your part of any doubts will be treated by your employees as a secret. You already know that that's a rule violation. This is particularly true if you've been gung ho in the opposite direction in the past. Just as damaging will be the effect that such doubts will have on the work-related activities of your own people. If the salespeople know you feel that the new marketing campaign is all wrong, they'll be inclined to slack off. Keep your doubts to yourself. If you need emotional reassurance, take it home or to a professional; don't give at the office.

Rule 77: Always foster the impression that senior management considers you and your department critical to the success of the organization.

If you always display a positive attitude and you don't express doubts to your employees, they'll feel good about themselves, the department, and you. It's important to foster the impression that your department is considered to be the vital cog in the organizational machine. Fortunately, this is a natural tendency in small groups. Foster and encourage it as much as you can. Be sure to pass along any positive remarks, compliments, or observations from management. Always phrase problems in the proper positive tone.

Bad: "Look, everyone, the brass is really mad about all the misdirected mail we've been sending out of here. They told me that if the mail room isn't shaped up fast, we're going to be in big trouble. So watch out, *or else!*"

First of all, if you're such a poor manager that you can't get a mail room shaped up, this book won't help you much; you have to have minimally acceptable technical skills in order to succeed in most careers. Secondly, this type of group talk is worthless. There's no need to get everyone worked up by airing out some nebulous threat. They don't need to know they're in trouble. All they need is for you to direct them to do better. If you were to give a group pep talk on the above problem (in addition to the more important individual counseling sessions you should conduct with the key or problem people), it should be phrased as follows.

Good: "Look, everyone, I was just upstairs in J.B.'s office, and he was telling me that he thinks the department is doing a great job. He told me that he appreciates your efforts to keep the organization's essential written communications moving.''

(Now everyone has a positive or at least a neutral feeling about what you're saying. Actually, J.B. had said, ''It's so screwed up down there, I suppose I should be grateful when half of them call in sick and stay home every day. It minimizes the trouble they can cause!'')

''J.B. also mentioned that he was concerned that we maintain our best efforts in the face of the increased work we've had to do lately. I was forced to admit to J.B. that, despite all the glowing reports, we have made a few mistakes lately and that we're having a little too much sick time but that we are working on ways to improve our service. In order to make sure that we stay in everyone's good graces, I'm going to be meeting with each of you over the course of the next few weeks to work on our systems. Thanks for the great job you've been doing.''

Wouldn't you feel good after getting a speech like that from your boss? You'd feel complimented, involved, and successful. There's no reason for all the employees to know that J.B. just about popped an artery in his neck while he was screaming about his personal mail being sent to the Sales department by mistake.

It's your job to get things fixed in the most effective way. Dumping your emotional garbage on your employees may make you feel better when they share the guilt, but it will decrease your department's effectiveness and cause you more trouble later. Then you'll have even more guilt to share the next time things go wrong. They're paying you for those big, broad manager's shoulders so that you can get the tough jobs done. Shielding your people from pointless abuse while you deal with the grief yourself is one of the toughest jobs you've got. So keep those positive comments going at all times.

Rule 78: Never attempt to fool your employees about the real intentions of the organization.

You're only human. There is only so much you can do. You may be able to maintain a positive low profile, follow all the rules about supervision, and do a great technical job for your organization, but you cannot get away with any really big lies to your employees. If your organization treats employees like disposable trashcan liners, you aren't going to be able to make them feel like they're working as personal assistants to Albert Schweitzer. You can, if you follow the rules carefully, get them to like working for you, to respect you, and even to work hard for you. But you won't be able to get them to like the company if it treats them badly. Don't try to do the impossible. No situation is 100 percent changeable or positive. If you try to change people's attitudes on clearly perceived issues, you can wind up losing your credibility in other ways. Don't risk it.

Rule 79: Your employees will quickly spot any differences between what you do and what you say.

In other words, don't be a hypocrite. A lot of managers are hypocrites, and everyone sees through the hypocrisy. Less work gets done, morale suffers, and the hypocrite managers lose respect as everyone ridicules them behind their backs. Some of the best ways to demonstrate that you're a complete hypocrite are the following.

Say: "Ms. Jones, official working hours are official working hours. I expect everyone to work their full schedule. Please try to get back from lunch on time, not five minutes late."

Then do: "Ms. Jones, I'll be in late tomorrow. I have to get my nine iron fixed at the pro shop."

Or: "Ms. Jones, cancel my appointments for Wednesday afternoon. J.B. and I are going to get in eighteen holes before we leave for the executive planning conference in the Bahamas."

Say: "I expect everyone to act like professional managers around here. Image and proper demeanor are critical."

Then do: In a departmental conference, refer to a member of the board as "that crazy guy with the cinnamon roll hair."

Or: Interrupt an entire meeting when a very attractive female comes in, with a comment such as, "You're really looking sexy today. I can hardly keep my hands off you!"

Say: "Look, Bob, when I ask you to be here for a 9:15 meeting, I expect you to be here at 9:15, not 9:17 or 9:18. Do you understand?"

Then do: Cancel with no notice, double book, or simply don't show up for 90 percent of all meetings with your people. Use "so busy that it slipped my mind" as an excuse.

Or: Start the meeting on time but then take all phone calls, including personal ones, that come in. Also, allow people without appointments to "stick their heads in just for a moment" and use up all the time. Then tell the poor slob who asked for the meeting that "we're out of time, but maybe we can get together next week."

Say: "We're on a tight budget here. We've got to tighten up. So I'm sorry, but we can't afford the dozen doughnuts you've been buying for the monthly working breakfasts you've been having with your department."

Then do: Allow higher-level executives to attend three-day out-of-state seminars at ski resorts in the winter and at beach resorts in the summer.

Or: Spend thousands of dollars to "upgrade" the office furniture of executives and high-level managers.

Say: "We're an aggressive company that demands creativity, independent decision making, and responsibility with authority from our people."

Then do: Create endless committees to decide every issue and shoot down any and all new ideas by saying, "Too much change is bad," and, "When I said creative, I didn't mean *that* different," or, "It's a great idea, but there's no budget for it."

Remember, there are no secrets (Rule 73) among your employees about anything you do. If one of them spots an inconsistency in your behavior, particularly if it runs counter to something you're really pushing, he or she will treat it as a secret, meaning that everybody will hear about it. You must carefully present a consistent and well-planned image.

Rule 80: There is no shame in your employees' knowing that you occasionally make mistakes.

A few little mistakes will make you seem all the more human and lovable. Since you will be projecting a rather cool, formal image by your careful rule following, the few small errors you're bound to make here and there can actually be helpful. They will give your employees the impression that you're a little like one of them, fallible just like they are. (Needless to say, you don't want to appear too much like them.) The disclosure of small, cute, nondemeaning errors will enable you to appear more human without the necessity for dangerous personal disclosures. For example, if you happen to put on one blue sock and one black one because you got dressed in the dark, don't worry about it. If someone notices it, just smile and say that they matched in the dark. It's a harmless little mistake that everyone can chuckle about and over which you'll lose little status. Conversely, you would not want to tell about the time that you woke up with a hangover after a party at a date's house, dressed, and drove all the way to work wearing your jockey shorts on the outside of your suit. That error has too many uncute, nonmastery aspects. Keep your disclosure of errors simple and unrelated to your technical work. If you make a big mistake on a piece of technical work, review your work processes if it happens more than once in a while. Don't announce any significant errors that you do make unless it can't be avoided (such as if your employees have to do a project over). There is no sense in appearing to be more fallible and human than necessary.

Rule 81: You must give your employees the opportunity to contribute and participate.

You're going to be evaluated to one degree or another on the overall performance of your department. You'll get optimum performance only if you have a dedicated and properly motivated group of employees. If your employees perceive that they are not an active, involved part of the decision-making process, they will work at much less than their capacity. Many managers do not understand this very simple point. Each and every employee believes that he or she has something to offer in the way of ideas and suggestions. It's true that a lot of the ideas and suggestions will be worthless in terms of content and real help (although if too many are that way, you'd better look for different people). That's OK. The very act of being listened to is satisfying to all of us. We all like to feel that someone is taking the time to listen to what we say, not because of the content but just because we are saying it. This listening builds group cohesion and motivation for the group to work together for common purposes.

Surveys of employees' attitudes routinely and consistently demonstrate that a lot of managers don't understand what most employees want from a job. Most managers rank pay, job security, and promotions as the things that employees are most concerned about. No wonder most managers won't be getting anywhere in life! The following job factors are those that are typically used in employee–supervisor attitude surveys. Note the differences between the rankings of supervisors and their employees about what's most important to the employees.

These general survey results are replicated almost exactly in every survey of this type across all industries for workers at all levels. It's the twentieth century; management approaches that worked 200 years ago just aren't going to cut it anymore. Workers expect a lot more from their jobs than money. If you, as a manager, don't provide some satisfaction of their nonmonetary needs, you're never going to get even a fraction of what your employees would give for a good manager. Without that extra effort, the managers who do it right are going to be way ahead of you.

Factor	Supervisors' rankings	Employees' rankings
Good pay	1	9
Job security	2	12
Promotion opportunities	3	10
Sense of achievement	8	1
Personal recognition	13	2
Leadership	12	3
Proper direction/training	11	4
Knowledge of what's expected	14	5

A word of warning: If you think you can just pretend to listen and then go off on your own, forget it. Remember, there are no secrets. If they catch you in this lie, you will have lost their respect forever. The most important reason to foster the participation of your employees is that you will never be able to delegate authority and work effectively unless your employees are genuinely involved. If you deny them a meaningful role, they'll only go through the motions and won't have a personal stake in seeing that things work out. A related benefit is that you will get a lot of ideas you might not have thought of. Everyone has a different perspective on a problem. Take what you can get; you're going to need it all to get to the top.

Rule 82: Deal with performance problems at the first sign of trouble.

Nothing gets better by just hoping about it. Occasionally the odds will work out that way, but the majority of the time a bad situation simply gets worse since most performance problems become self-perpetuating. If you notice one of your employees doing something that's just a little improper, incorrect, or irregular, deal with it immediately. If the employee's actions are not corrected by some outside influence, the employee will either notice that he or she is getting away with something or assume that the way he or she did it is OK. In either case, you have the beginnings of what could turn out to be a major problem down the road. It's much easier and a lot less painful to invest a little time at the moment and make sure that things are straightened out immediately. You are not doing the employee a favor if you wait to deal with the problem. Later, it will just be bigger, and the corrective procedures or reprimand from you will have to be proportionately larger. Simply take the employee aside at the first opportunity and explain exactly what you observed (or what you believe occurred, if you weren't there when it happened). Tell the employee why you are displeased and then outline exactly the behaviors you want to see in the future. If you do it nicely and in a positive manner, it won't be too unpleasant to the employee. For example, Mr. Norton, a manager in Sales, noticed that Eustace, a salesman, hadn't been getting in on time every day. Otherwise, Eustace was doing OK.

> *Mr. Norton:* "Have a seat, Eustace. Say, your sales last week looked pretty good. How's it going with the Mullins account? Do you think we can work our way in as a full-line widget supplier? J.B. is particularly interested in any progress."
>
> (Here Mr. Norton is starting off the discussion on a positive note and getting some relevant business data that he needs. Do not waste too much time beating around the bush with nonsense; keep the discussion on business items of importance. If you deal with trivia and then reprimand the employee, the employee either will perceive that you were insincere in your initial remarks or will think that you didn't have the nerve to get tough.)
>
> *Eustace:* "Well, the account's going good...."
>
> *Mr. Norton:* "Well, that's good. I'll pass the word along to J.B. I want you to do me a favor, Eustace."
>
> *Eustace:* "Sure. What is it?"
>
> *Mr. Norton:* "You're getting off to a pretty good start here at ABC Company. I'd hate to see anything compromise your fine efforts. I've noticed that you've been getting in a little late two or three

days a week. People talk about that sort of thing, and it makes you look bad. I'd like to see you in here by 8:00 every day. Can you handle that?''

Mr. Norton handled it pretty well. He asked Eustace for a favor and then told him what he wanted in specific terms and why he wanted it. If you let it ride, things will get more unpleasant, and you may wind up with a situation that causes you to lose some of your credibility. Good employees can quickly turn into bad employees under a bad or careless manager. And once they go bad, it's almost impossible to shape them up without a lot of bad press and grousing.

Rule 83: Never give more chances to one employee than to another.

Your employees will respect you and work hard for you if you treat them fairly and with courtesy and respect. The key word here is *fairly*. Even the most abusive tyrant gets off pretty easily if he or she is equally mean and rotten to everyone. If you are perceived as being more tolerant of one employee than another, you will lose the respect of your people. Worse, they will begin to see that your standards are not as rigid as you stated them to be. Once you are perceived as having elastic performance standards, your people will start to make their own determinations of how to do things. You'll then have to bear down like a despot to get things back under control. Equal treatment is especially important in regard to an organization's general policies. Special treatment in regard to days off, arrival and departure times, vacations, and general office demeanor will be recognized instantly by other employees. It doesn't matter if the reasons behind your exceptions are justified. Everyone can think up fifty good excuses for why they should get to come in late, take extra days off, and so on. You have to be tough when it comes to granting special exemptions from established policies.

Rule 84: Never be more understanding and progressive than the organization permits.

Some organizations are extremely open, flexible, and progressive in terms of how far a manager can go in setting policies and standards for his or her own employees and in granting independence to them. In most organizations, there are unwritten laws about how independent and even how nice a manager can be before he or she is considered different or "soft." Make sure you understand your organization's stance in this area before you try to be super progressive. I once worked with a very capable manager who was having all sorts of success in increasing productivity and morale among his seventy employees in a large paper and data processing department. He had instituted flextime, worker participation incentive systems, contests, bonuses of time off and cash for top-producing individuals and sections, and a number of extra in-house luncheon programs for the whole department. Under his direction, productivity increased 32 percent, unexcused absences and sick time decreased 22 percent, and overall costs for the department decreased 12 percent.

One day, the grizzled, bullet-shaped executive VP (who started in the mail room) visited the department with a few potential clients. The executive VP knew nothing about the operations of the department or the steps that had been taken to clean things up; he only knew that results were better. As the executive VP was standing in the middle of the department with the prospects, a whole section of the department walked in, took off their coats, and moved to their work stations. The executive VP asked why all these employees were arriving for work at 10:30 in the morning. One of the supervisors explained that this section had elected to work a 10:30 A.M. to 7:00 P.M. shift in order to avoid rush-hour traffic. The VP was told that the policy permitted them to select their own hours as long as they were present during the "core" hours of 11:00 A.M. to 4:00 P.M. As soon as the prospects were sent off to lunch with the VP of Sales, the executive VP called the manager and his boss, the VP of Operations, into his office and demanded to know "what all this nonsense was, with workers setting their own hours and all." He was enraged that "standard company policy was not being followed." Explanations were offered, and productivity and cost data were presented, but to no avail. As the executive VP stated, "I'm surprised that you don't understand how badly this hurts the company. We just don't do things like that around here." In that organization, all decisions of substance were made at the top. As long as it did not appear that a manager was challenging authority, he or she could get away with anything, including gross incompetence. But even the most exceptional performance was severely and swiftly punished if it was found in the presence of the least little bit of independent decision making. Three months after the above incident, my progressive peer was replaced during a reorganization, and a "company man" was put in charge. Three months after that, the department was in more disarray than ever before; turnover and costs were up, productivity was down, and clients were no longer shown through the department. But the new manager was doing a "great job." Just ask his boss, the executive VP. The moral of this sad, typical tale: Don't be more progressive than the organization can tolerate (and it can't tolerate much).

Rule 85: If you have a chronically poor performer, do everyone a favor and get rid of him or her.

One poor performer, whether in the technical end of the job or in the supervisory end, can ruin the best efforts of everyone else. One visible poor performer can ruin the effects of all your other rule following. Once you have attempted corrective efforts with an employee and they have failed, do not hesitate to take the next step: to get rid of or isolate the problem. Any delay will inflict more damage to your overall efforts. If an employee is not receptive to corrective measures, that employee's attitude will be like a dangerous cancer. The efforts of other employees will be ruined or their own attitudes will be influenced by the bad-mouthing of the troublemaker. Even more damaging is the fact that good employees will feel that they are being taken advantage of because they'll have to live with the bad press and do the extra work that their colleague isn't doing. Be prepared to move fast at the earliest possible opportunity after it is clear that your salvage attempts have failed. Once an employee knows he or she is in trouble with the boss and feels that it's someone else's fault, the employee will spread more bad news than a public health reporter during a plague. Quick steps on your part will demonstrate to the other employees that you will not tolerate troublemakers and that you are deadly serious about everyone working together as a team. The good workers will be grateful for your efforts.

Rule 86: Do not allow your own feelings of guilt and/or insecurity to prevent you from taking unpleasant employee-related actions.

Most of us know what it's like to be fired. And most of us know what it is like to be reprimanded, deservedly and otherwise. Unless you have a rather bizarre personality, you don't enjoy having to fire or discipline your employees. Whether you enjoy it or not, sometimes it has to be done, and you're the one who has to do it. When the time comes, don't allow your emotions to postpone what you know has to be done. Even more importantly, don't allow your emotions to play havoc with your own mental state. It's natural to feel some guilt and/or anxiety when something unpleasant has to be done. We'd all like to be able to do more, whether it's for our families, our employees, or society. We all feel various degrees of guilt about not doing enough. There's not much you can do about these feelings other than to acknowledge them and then keep on going. It's OK to admit to yourself that firing someone is a bad scene and that you wish you didn't have to do it. That's a healthy normal reaction as long as you keep it to yourself. You aren't going to solve the world's problems by taking them on at work. Your mission is to take the best action for your career and for your organization, in that order. If you follow the rules and manage your employees and yourself fairly and knowledgeably, it's not your fault if someone has to be chastised or fired. Carry out your unpleasant duties with as much consideration as possible, and you'll be doing all that anyone could expect. You can't do more than that, and most people do a lot less.

Rule 87: Remember that understanding may be interpreted as weakness.

This is particularly true in a production-oriented environment or in an organization where management is already perceived as "big brother." In such conditions, you would be wise to be very careful about being too understanding or flexible with individual employees or situations. You've got two audiences to be concerned with in this regard: your superiors and your employees. Employees are continually testing the limits that their supervisors and the organization establish. Even the good workers will be constantly probing to find out how much more independence and autonomy they can get. You've got to be extremely careful when you ease up on any of the many sets of reins you hold. Any easing of the controls, guidelines, or standards may be viewed as an indication of your lack of strength. Workers who are chronic complainers or borderline performers will be especially difficult if they think it's possible to get away with something. Even if you're motivated solely out of concern for their development as better workers, you'll lose big for both them and yourself if you let them get away with even the smallest deviation that's not in line with your carefully planned image development. The next time, the oversight will be bigger. When you finally call them on it (and you'll eventually have to because it's natural for employees to stretch tolerance to the limits and then some), they'll be shocked and angry and may run to management, the union, or other workers with tales of your inconsistency and unfairness. It gets out of hand *fast*. Do not have misplaced compassion when it's not appropriate (meaning when it can't help your career).

It's just as critical to make sure that your bosses perceive that you're just as tough as they are in regard to employee supervision. The very same executive who lets his or her secretary come in late and leave early all the time will view you as a weakling if you let your secretary work through lunch so that he or she can leave an hour early to pick up a child at the day-care center. This is a different issue from that of violations of company policy (as discussed in Rule 83). Here the concern is for you to appear just as ruthless as the executives like to think they are. Many think they are very ruthless. As they die off and top management becomes a little more enlightened about how to get the most out of workers, softness (meaning doing whatever is necessary to optimize productivity, including things that "weren't done in my day") in dealing with employees may become the norm. But no matter what the orientation of your organization's executives in regard to handling employees, it's critical for you to appear to march in step with them.

Rule 88: Never discuss the performance problem of a worker within earshot of persons who are not involved in the evaluation process.

It's your job to objectively assess and evaluate the performance of your workers. This information can then be shared with appropriate individuals who also participate in your organization's evaluation system (personnel analysts, your supervisor, and so on). It is no one else's business except the employee who is the object of the discussion. Other employees and even your management colleagues cannot function as impartial listeners. They all have axes to grind, and they may decide at some future point that they can get the best edge on theirs by sharpening it on your neck. You can never tell where the information will go once you share it with an inappropriate person. For example, suppose you were to tell a colleague that a particular employee of yours isn't doing too well and you'd like to get rid of him. A month later, you might find that the employee had applied for a transfer to your colleague's department, and the slot goes with him. The other manager slicked you by having a confidential chat with the employee about your attitude and his probable tenure. By the time the proposal got to you, the brass were already convinced it was a good move. You'd be out the slot, and the new manager could then get rid of the person after a decent interval and bring in a good worker.

Particularly dangerous are off-hand comments made in anger about one employee in front of several others. Your remarks, however justified, will be gleefully distorted and then reported to the employee in question by departmental troublemakers. (Those few individuals who follow the rules will keep their mouths shut, but you can't count on many of them being in any one company.) Any chance you may have had to straighten out the employee will be lost once he or she has been humiliated in the eyes of the others. Worse yet, you may be wrong. The bottom line is that you must never make comments about the problems of an employee outside the performance appraisal system. Of course, positive observations about employees' performances should be made liberally within earshot of everyone. They will travel almost as fast as bad comments, will serve as powerful rewards for the good performers, and may function as guilt generators for some of the marginal employees.

Rule 89: Always foster the impression that you possess total and complete hire-and-fire authority over your employees.

If you are following the appropriate rules, your employees will come to perceive you as the one for whom they are working, rather than the organization as a whole. You must encourage this view by reinforcing their beliefs that you possess total authority over their futures. Of course you don't, but that is irrelevant. Most employees have extremely distorted impressions about the relative power possessed by various management people. They almost always overestimate the amount of power that is held by their own managers as well as that which is held by the organization's officers. You can use this misconception for your own purposes. For example, never say, "Personnel will have to decide on this one." Instead, say, "I'll discuss it with Personnel and see what we can work out." If the decision goes against you, you can always phrase it in such a way as to make it look like you were forced to give in to legal or organizational guidelines rather than admitting that they overruled you.

The goal here is not to distort reality in order to boost your ego, but to motivate your employees to work for you and worry about your assessments, rather than those of the organization's vast bureaucracy.

Rule 90: Establish only those reward systems in which you are the evaluator and the distributor of the rewards.

If you are to manage most effectively, your employees will have to perceive that you are the one they must satisfy. If you are going to establish additional reward systems, make sure that you are the one who determines what the rewards will be and how performance will be assessed. Even more importantly, you must be the one who distributes the rewards. Do not believe that it is beneath your dignity to distribute Worker of the Month pins or the like. The very fact that you are the one doing the presenting is very helpful to establishing that you are the one they work for. Of course, if the Worker of the Month contest is a big joke, work to get rid of it or at least the presentation honors if that is safe. If you establish any kind of charting (behavior modification) system at all, make sure you are the one who determines the performance standards, not the employees. You wouldn't let a two-year-old decide on the criteria for being good, would you? Well, then don't let even more clever adults set up the criteria by which they will be rewarded. It's OK and desirable to let them participate in setting goals and procedures for improving efficiency, but you must be the one who is the final yes or no authority. The problem with most incentive systems is that there is little direct perceived relationship between the rewarder, the reward, and the required performance. If you set the performance standards and determine the rewards, you'll be effectively eliminating the two most common problem areas encountered in work environment incentive systems.

Don't let the above convince you that you should join the stampede to run with the behavior-modification, incentive-system herd. Most of the time, it's possible to get big increases in productivity from employees simply by managing them consistently and intelligently. Before you try anything heroic (and getting a good incentive system to work is a heroic act), read Rule 66 and Appendix D several times. You might decide to get by without a new incentive system.

Rule 91: Do not be too liberal with rewards and praise.

It is a basic law of learning that individuals will work harder for more infrequent rewards. Infrequent rewards will also result in learning (habits) that is more resistant to outside influences. You want your employees to work harder for the praise and other rewards you give them (attention, more independence, more responsibility). But you can't start them off with only rarely given praise and expect it to work. At first, when trying to correct or establish a desired behavior in a given employee, it's necessary to give lots of praise or rewards each time the desired behavior occurs.

Smart boss: "John, I noticed that you got in here fifteen minutes early today. I want you to know I appreciate your businesslike attitude and your concern for our work load."

John had been getting in late every morning, and the boss had to have an attitude adjustment session in which she told John that she expected him to be on time or else he would not receive a positive performance review, which would hurt his chances for an upcoming chance at a promotion. The smart boss realizes that you must begin a reward schedule with frequent and easily earned rewards. After giving several almost immediate reinforcements for a number of John's good behaviors over the course of a week or so, the smart boss begins to "thin" the reinforcement schedule.

Smart boss: "John, I've been noticing that you've been getting in here so early during this last week that you've had the coffee made before I got here. You're setting a good example for the others. Keep up the good work!"

This smart boss is really smart. Not only does she make the reward a little more difficult (John had to get in early for several days in order to earn it), but she makes the reward bigger (admitting that John beat her to work and that it's setting an example for the others). If a boss does not begin to "thin" his or her employees' reward schedules in order to maintain the desired behaviors with fewer "attaboys," he or she would spend a good part of the week doing nothing besides giving out rewards for every little behavior. You don't have the time to do that if you're taking care of other business. Be parsimonious with your praise; it'll work better.

Rule 92: Never promise or suggest rewards that have not been officially approved.

What seems reasonable, straightforward, and even essential to you may seem like a total crock to your boss or to some nitpicker in Personnel or Corporate. Don't assume that your requests, suggestions, or programs will be approved. Don't promise or suggest bonuses, extra privileges, salary increases, or anything until you have received absolute, final written confirmation that the action has been approved by every last relevant cog in the bureaucratic gear train. If you jump the gun and tell an employee that an increase or a promotion is set, I guarantee that you'll walk in the next day and get a call from someone in Personnel that will ruin your plans. If you shoot your mouth off too soon, you'll be faced with the unpleasant task of informing the employee that the promised goodies are not going to arrive. You'll feel like an idiot, and you will have earned the title. The employee's morale will be shot. You can never be sure that an action will get approved simply because it was approved before or because it makes good business sense.

When I was first starting out in the business world, I had my morale crushed by a boss who performed the all too common ploy of promising an increase before checking and then not giving it. I was working in my first postcollege job as a management trainee for a prominent retail chain while I attended graduate school at night. I was so happy to be in the "business world" that I was considering the abandonment of my "professional" career in favor of a career in retailing. After about a year in the job, I was offered a position by another retailer at a modest salary increase. I went to my boss and told him about the offer. I told him that I didn't want to take it but that I needed the money. I pointed out that I had not received an increase since I had joined the company but had been promoted once. He said there was no problem. I turned down the job offer and eagerly awaited my first pay raise. Two weeks later I got my next paycheck, and, you guessed it, there was no increase. I went to my boss and asked him what the delay was. He said, "There's no delay. You can't have the increase. I didn't realize you were already making so much. The merchandise manager says that I can't give you any more. Sorry." I was getting a lousy $135 per week, putting in extra time, and working every Saturday and three nights per week. That experience soured me on a retail career, and I quit as soon as I found a position in another field. This sort of thing is done every day by managers who act impulsively. Don't let it happen to you. The personal needs of individuals, the political environment, and even the cast changes from day to day in most organizations. The same conditions never exist from one day to the next.

Rule 93: Do not be reluctant to praise a bad worker for a good behavior or to reprimand a good worker for a mistake.

Very often, managers have more trouble with the little mistakes and problems of good workers than with the prototypical shiftless bum. After all, you can get rid of a worker who is bad enough, but you hate to alienate an otherwise good worker for a minor problem. Well, if you handle it properly, you can give the good worker the appropriate reprimand without creating new problems. The key is to deal only with specific problem behaviors. For example, suppose you have an otherwise good worker who keeps getting back from lunch late. Many managers would be reluctant to say anything. After all, what if the employee gets mad and it affects her work? And so what if she's a little late? Her work is so much better than most of the others, so why bother? You might get the good worker upset and ruin everything. Yet you feel guilty because you're worried that the other workers will spot your lax behavior toward the good worker's disobedience. You're afraid the other workers will see it and won't realize (or care) that the good worker produces more than they do. You're worried that if you let the good worker come in late, everyone will start to come in late, and then you'll be stuck with a major morale problem when you crack down. Well, you're right about the other workers' most likely reaction to perceived laxity for one employee. If they see it, they'll try to get away with it, too.

But that's not why you feel guilty. The guilt is generated by your recognition that you probably aren't reprimanding anybody for anything. Face it, you're letting almost anything get by unless it's pretty major. You see all sorts of little abuses of rules and regulations every day, and you let them go, not because they may be trivial and you could care less, but because you're afraid to be a real boss and give out a little grief. So you're letting it all build up inside you, and you're getting frustrated. There's only one way to handle it. You've got to take control of your management duties and do what has to be done. If someone— a good worker or a bum—does something that you don't like, speak up. If you stick to only the behaviors in question and make no value judgments about the employee's intentions or worth as a person, you'll have no problem (other than initial uneasiness), even with a good employee. Note how the smart boss handles it.

Smart boss: "Mary, almost every day you've been getting back from lunch a little late. I'd like you to give it a little more attention and try to keep it to one hour."

Mary: "Aren't you happy with my work?"

Smart boss: "Yes, your work is outstanding, and you'll get all the recognition for it that you deserve. I value your efforts, and you're an outstanding performer, but these late lunches don't look good. They compromise all the other hard work that you do by setting a bad example for other employees who don't know about your contributions."

Note that the smart boss didn't make the common but dangerous mistake of trying to tell Mary that he understood her intentions by saying, "Well, it's clear that you don't think it's important to get back on time." Don't try to interpret the whys or the hows of an employee's behavior. Just deal with the behavior itself and what you want to see in the future. If you've been doing your job as a supervisor, that should end it. If you haven't been doing your job, Mary would most likely respond with the following type of comment.

Mary: "Yeah, but I do make more contributions than the others. I've been staying late, working Saturdays when necessary, and even taking work home. I don't get paid any more than they do, but they come in late just as often as I do, and they don't do the extra work, and you're jumping on me. I don't see why I should keep doing more than they are if I'm going to be treated just like them."

Mary has a point there, especially since she's a secretary and is probably not going anywhere up in the organization. She's not going to get anything but self-satisfaction for her efforts. Even if you don't get this response verbally, it's there. The only way to avoid such nasty scenes (and the even nastier impact on your low profile) is to be scrupulously fair in your distribution of reprimands and praise. Start doing your job of supervising, and you'll avoid these problems. And don't be afraid to praise troublemakers for the occasional, rare, good job. Who knows; it may turn them around a little.

Rule 94: Give clear, detailed instructions and deadlines for any responsibilities you assign.

More often than we like to admit, we are the reason why our employees don't get a job done correctly or on time. We tend to view the world from our own personal viewpoint. We often assume that all others hold the same general orientation. They don't. If you doubt this, try a simple experiment. The next time you've finished giving instructions or presenting information to a group, ask each person to write down exactly what you said. You'll be unpleasantly surprised at the breadth of difference between peoples' perceptions of what you said and what you thought you said. The key to avoiding this very common problem is to make sure that you assign responsibilities in operational terms. This means that you have to specify exactly what behaviors each person must do and not just what kind of general results you want.

Vague: "I want this group to turn out a new product proposal that'll knock their socks off. We've got to get it done fast, and I want each of you to contribute in your specialty areas."

This sounds nice, but who cares? Instead, you should phrase your orders in strictly operational terms.

Clear: "This proposal has to be done in two weeks. I want it on my desk for first-draft review by next Thursday morning at 9:00. Jim, you write Chapter 1 on general market conditions. Sally, you're responsible for the Chapter 2 financial forecasts. Bob, you do Chapter 3, which will be the cost proposal. Mary, you write the maintenance and customer service sections and then jam into the usual boilerplate in Chapter 4. Pete, you're responsible for getting everyone's input, organizing it, and getting it word-processed. if anyone has any questions, see me after the meeting."

These are operational instructions. In some environments, your operationalized instructions will have to be more detailed. In others— especially groups that function well, have worked together for some time, or turn out a lot of the same stuff time after time—you can be more general because everyone will operationalize your orders for themselves. Take nothing for granted. Assign specific responsibilities and deadlines to the extent necessary to avoid any misunderstandings and to reduce opportunities for people to shift the responsibility for nonperformance.

Rule 95: Compliment each of your workers at least once a week for something that was done correctly and well.

Forget about behavior modification and reinforcement theory as a reason for telling your workers that they've done something right. The act of telling them accomplishes several very important things in addition to any direct effect on the behavior for which you compliment them. Your presence alone increases group morale and makes the individual worker feel good. You're around to see what's going on, and you're highly visible to any executives who may be in the area. If you can't find one good thing to say about each employee once a week, either you're not doing your job or the employees involved are unsalvageable. It's easy to get into a rut, even if it's a good one where everything is going along fine and you're in total control. You can't afford to assume that everybody is doing a good job because they all appear to like their work, seem to be happy with the pay, appear to be optimistic about the future, and don't seem to be reporting major problems. Once you start acting in accordance with this attitude, you'll begin to become lax about providing the constant positive flow of encouragement that all good leaders must provide if they want things to stay good. Don't believe that the organizational rewards (paychecks, benefits, and so on) are enough to keep your employees working at the pace you need. Paychecks are notoriously bad reinforcers; they come too regularly and too far apart and are not perceived as being directly tied to performance on a day-to-day basis (the kind of performance you are most concerned about). Your employees depend on immediate feedback from you, their peers, and the general situation (sales, morale, and so on) to determine how they are doing. You must provide positive feedback in order to show that you are watching, that you recognize good work, and that you are grateful for their efforts. The only way to make sure that you do this in a consistent pattern amidst all the pressures of day-to-day operations is to get into the habit of doing it regularly. Your good intentions aren't worth anything if you only get around to passing out strokes every couple of months. You've got to pass them out consistently and fairly. Set up a schedule if you must, but do it. It's essential that your compliments be real. If you fake it and just go through the motions, you'll end up doing more harm than good when the ones who deserve it see that everybody is getting strokes and view you as a plastic, insincere hypocrite.

Rule 96: Never ask your employees to perform personal chores for you.

Unless it's an emergency (like your car broken down on the freeway) or you're incredibly wealthy and have body servants and personal secretaries assigned to these tasks, don't expect or ask employees to perform personal services for you. I once worked as a manager in a division of a large conglomerate where there was a secretary who complained almost daily about the fact that one of the directors had made her sit in the gas lines with his car during the 1973 oil embargo. It was apparent by the frequency and tone of her grousings that she deeply resented having been made to perform this personal task. Every new employee heard the sad tale of woe and was exposed to her vitriolic descriptions of the director's character. When I first heard the story, it was six years after the fact! She was violating all sorts of rules, but she couldn't hold it in. Almost daily, the same director was assigning her and other secretarial and clerical personnel to fetch his dry cleaning, balance his checking account, pick up his kids, and so on. A few individuals had refused to perform these types of tasks. They quickly became the objects of blatant pressure to get out of the department. This director was one of the sleaziest businesspeople I have ever met. Nonetheless, all of his tasteless tales of sexual conquests on business trips, his blatant and obvious abuse of his expense account, and his gropings of female employees were viewed with less outrage than the fact that he used employees to perform his personal duties.

Each worker, whatever the role, prefers to think that he or she is a professional. By asking them to perform personal chores for you, you make a joke of their supposed professionalism. If they refuse to do what you ask, you are faced with an unpleasant situation. They'll be angry with you for asking and will always remember that you felt it was more important for your shirts to get picked up than for them to do their job. If they do what you ask, and even if they enjoy it (out of the mistaken belief that you are trusting them more), other workers will see it and you will pay with heavy attacks on your general reputation. Remember, an operative foundation of many of the rules is to maintain a low profile and to minimize the amount of your personal life that you expose at work. You can't do this and still have your assistant balancing your checkbook.

Rule 97: Always give salary and performance reviews on time.

Nothing smacks of hypocrisy more than an employee being told how "valuable" he or she is and how "appreciated" he or she is and then experiencing big delays in receiving performance reviews and any accompanying salary adjustments. Employees are very deeply upset with any more than a minor delay in receiving performance reviews, particularly if such reviews are normally followed by compensation increases. Yet many managers are chronically late in administering such reviews. If you are one of these managers, you've already lost the respect of your employees, and it will be difficult to win it back. Why should they push a little harder for you when you don't show them the most basic respect to their pocketbook? All sorts of reasons are given for these delays by the offending managers, but the real reasons are very simple:

1. The managers know that they've been doing a poor job of supervising their employees, they know that the employees know, and they don't want to be faced with the task of pointing out the plusses and minuses of each employee's performance after having let things slide all year.
2. The managers claim that they're "too busy" with more important things.

Number one is the primary reason why managers generally fail to get performance reviews moving from their end. It's a pointless strategy because it just increases the anxiety. If you're not going to do your job as a manager the way you should, why increase your anxiety by getting everybody more upset? You know the reviews will have to be done eventually. It's going to be harder to conduct them if the employee has to wait three months and then finds out that the pay increase isn't retroactive. Good luck on getting more work out of them. Number two is, of course, total rubbish. The most important thing a manager does is to optimize his or her employees' performance.

The biggest part of that role is giving regular and honest performance-related feedback to each employee. Performance reviews are an integral part of such feedback because of their visibility and relationship to compensation. If you don't have the time for that, you're not doing your job properly. After all, that's how you really manage your employees. If you really are too busy to get to the paperwork and it's not your fault, it's time for you to move on and find an organization that doesn't stack things so heavily against aspiring successes and devoted rule followers.

Rule 98: Never compromise official work hours.

If you do this, you'll be opening the floodgates to a torrent of abuse from all quarters. Generally, your employees' hours are set by company standards. Although this may seem like a major disadvantage when you're snuggled deep in your bed on a cold morning and would like to dally in the sack another hour, in reality your organization is doing you a favor. I guarantee you that if you begin to allow even one employee to begin stretching lunch or coming in ten minutes late in the morning, soon everyone will be doing it. The end results will be that you will have seriously undermined your position as the leader. The employees will perceive that, in this area, they are their own leaders. Even more damaging to you personally will be the fact that other managers, your supervisors, and other departments' employees will recognize what is going on. Your reputation will be sorely tarnished. Hold your people firmly to the official starting times, lunch hours, and quitting times right from the start. It'll save you a lot of trouble.

Rule 99: Do not expect your employees to put in a lot of extra unpaid time.

As a highly motivated member of management (or an aspiring one), you recognize that it is sometimes necessary to put in a lot of unpaid time—that is, time that won't be directly compensated in your next paycheck. In the long run, of course, we all expect such extra efforts to pay off in increased earnings, success, larger offices, personal achievement, and so on. If we didn't think there would be some payoff, however delayed, we wouldn't make what appear to be sacrifices in the here and now. As a result, many of us have put in the standard weekend trips to Chicago in the winter to review last-minute programs, we have sat in on endless Saturday morning executive committee meetings (held on weekends to allow the executives to show what sacrifices they make), and we have burned up many hours by hanging around the office long enough in the evening to convince our bosses that we're real go-getters. Most of the population does not share this long-term approach to putting in extra uncompensated time. And you can't expect them to feel otherwise. There is only so much room at the top, and more people than you think know that they aren't going to make it. A lot of them don't even think it's worth the try. So they don't try. They work for the paycheck, and then they go bowling, fishing, camping, drinking, and so on, for their personal satisfaction. Do not apply your own standards to these types of people; you will alienate them. They will work hard, but they have very absolute limits on what they feel are appropriate justifications for intrusions into their own time. If there is an emergency, you should expect them to pitch in willingly. As a routine policy, don't expect to get away with it and to maintain their respect, support, and productivity. If you impose upon them with too many emergencies, you'll lose your credibility. Not everybody is willing to make significant sacrifices for their success, much less yours. Always keep this in mind when asking for extras from your troops.

Rule 100: Never permit your employees to develop relationships with your superiors.

Be honest with yourself. Don't you sometimes wish that you had a direct line to the CEO or the president's office so that you could tell it like it is, cut out all the garbage, and get something done for a change? This is true even though you now know that such moves are dangerous and stupid; nobody wants to hear it, and you'll only attract the wrong kind of attention. The problem is that many of the people who work for you still harbor this same fantasy. In their ignorance, they would love nothing more than to develop a direct line around you so they could avoid all of your garbage and get something done for a change. Keep a careful eye on your people if they show signs of coming down with the executive suite syndrome. Once they catch it, your career may come down with a high fever.

Some misguided and incompetent executives will actually encourage these types of relationships because they think they'll get a lot of real insight into what's really going on by talking with the troops. What they'll get will be nothing but the sour-grape translations of some axe-grinding troublemaker. But they'll most likely think it's good information. If these types of executives were doing their real job (planning and guiding), they wouldn't have time to listen to such nonsense. Since they can't manage by guiding and directing their own employees, they do it by trying to find all the problems and coming down hard on those who appear most responsible. Such an approach requires little business acumen and no planning. Your employees, particularly the borderline ones, will be glad to point out all the "serious problems" they've noticed if they get a turn at an executive earflap. Don't permit it. Make it perfectly clear to everyone that you are the sole contact with your superiors and that your boss doesn't want to be bothered by every Tom, Dick, and Harriet who is lower on the organization ladder. Most organizations have rather strong feelings about chain of command. If necessary, use the organizational authority to crack down on such types. Tell them that you'll write them up for insubordination if they go around you. You must always hide your true concern and couch your reprimand in terms that point out your concern for policies, procedures, and the most efficient use of executives' time.

This method can be effective even if a certain executive is encouraging one of your employees. If worse comes to worst and you can't shut down the relationship, you may have to tactfully move the employee out. Subordinates who get involved in these relationships begin to think that they are special. They start to believe that they can get away with all sorts of abuses because they feel that they can run upstairs if someone gives them grief. If they get in so tight that they're protected, you're in big trouble, particularly if you haven't been a good rule follower; they'll have lots to report. Luckily, it usually takes quite a while for someone in the ranks to develop such a relationship; there's a lot of natural executive suspicion to overcome. If you keep your eyes open, you'll be able to spot employees who attempt to cultivate relationships with executives before they get in too tight. The key is to move fast when you discover such attempts. Nail them for the little things if they don't respond to your suggestions about proper reporting lines. The one consolation is that if you are consistently following all of the rules, you'll be safe from the damage that such a relationship could cause a careless manager. Except for wholesale lies, the employee will have nothing to distort or misinterpret during the "dumping" sessions with the executive. But there's no need to take chances by letting it get to that point. Make it clear that you will not tolerate this type of behavior.

8

Making the Rules Work for You: A Self-Improvement Program

You've read the rules, you've had the benefit of being exposed to a different and enlightening perspective of the work world, and perhaps you've had a few insights into some of your less than successful day-to-day behaviors at work. Maybe you've even had a few laughs at some of your standard behaviors and those of your colleagues and bosses. Well, the fun part is over. The question at this point is, "Just what are you going to do about what you've learned?" If you think you can just sort of keep the rules in mind while you're walking around at work and thereby improve your odds of success, you're out of luck. Just knowing about something isn't enough.

Now that you know what to do, you're not any better off than before. In fact, you may be even worse off if you don't do anything with your new knowledge. Unless you do something, you'll still make the same old blunders. Since you'll know they're errors, you'll get down on yourself and most likely make even more mistakes out of frustration and impatience. So what do you do? If you want to get moving with that mess you've been embarrassed to call a career, you put the rules to work by embarking on modest behavior modification program in which you're both the subject and the experimenter.

It's not a major undertaking, and it's not a big hassle like a lot of self-improvement programs. You've probably read about diet, smoking, and exercise behavior modification programs that require hours of point totaling, graph drawing, and journal keeping. Most of the time, the paperwork is included solely to impress the neophyte with the complexity of the system. You don't need or want that kind of garbage. You're already motivated to be successful, or you wouldn't have read this book. The elements of a self-behavior modification program are very simple. The difficult part is having the self-control and the discipline to make yourself spend the ten or fifteen minutes a day it will take to analyze each day's performance. It's not much time, but it's like everything else we know we should do for ourselves; as soon as a momentary crisis or something that appears more important occurs, we let it slide. Pretty soon, the "absolutely no exceptions, thirty-minute jog every day" becomes a fifteen-minute event once or twice a week and then gets dropped because "it's not doing any good." This program is no different. If you are serious about putting the rules to work, it's a good idea to read the appendices before putting this chapter's program into effect. This chapter outlines a practical, step-by-step program for self-behavior modification. The appendices will provide you with the whys behind the workings of social psychology, group and organization behavior, and behavior modification programs in a work setting.

The most critical element in a self-improvement program is feedback. You have to have a means of objectively reviewing your behaviors so that you can congratulate yourself for your successes and direct more attention to your shortcomings. If you were designing and implementing a behavior modification program for another person or animal, you'd be operating under some restrictions that don't apply when you're working on yourself. With other people as your subjects, you'd have to limit the targets of the program to overt, observable behaviors, since you can never be sure what other people or animals are thinking. With yourself as a subject, you can consider your own attitudes and thoughts as legitimate behaviors (you know when you're feeling sorry for yourself, and you know when you've had a thought that the organization will take care of you). An even greater advantage of working on yourself occurs in terms of feedback. When you're working with young children or animals, the feedback usually has to be a primary reinforcement such as candy or access to toys. When you implement a practical behavior modification program at work for other employees, you usually have to go to a lot of trouble to design a system of secondary social reinforcements in which the various groups provide social reinforcements ("attaboys") to group members who perform the desired behaviors. It's hard to get such a system going and to maintain it in the face of day-to-day operational pressures. With yourself as the subject of the behavior modification program, you don't have that problem. You'll give yourself pats on the back for performing the desired behaviors or thoughts; your reinforcements will come from your own feelings of achievement, self-satisfaction, and pride. These are the same feelings you get when you step on the scale and see that you've been successful in losing three pounds. Nobody has to tell you that you did well; you know it and feel good about it. The self-improvement program in this chapter works on the same principle.

The system is very simple. The last part of this chapter presents a number of feedback charts (FCs). Each of the FCs deals with a specific performance area, such as "Boss Management and Executive Relations" (FC 4). Table 1 lists the various FCs and the respective areas of performance on which each concentrates.

You use the FCs to evaluate your behaviors (including attitudes and feelings) on a regularly scheduled basis. It's not as overpowering as it appears. Although there are thirteen pages of FCs and a total of 139 items against which to check your performance, it's not necessary to review all of them on a daily basis. For example, it's clearly not necessary to conduct a daily review of FC 1 every day; once a week is sufficient. You'll find that it's pretty quick and easy to score your behavior on each of the items. After using them a few times, it shouldn't take more than

Table 1. Feedback Chart Items and Subject Areas

Feedback chart number	Number of pages	Number of performance items	Performance area
1	2	19	Your view of yourself and the world
2	2	19	Your attitudes and behaviors about work, organizations, your job, and coworkers
3	3	32	General demeanor
4	3	31	Boss management and executive relations
5	3	29	Employee supervision

five minutes to go through the entire set of FCs. Table 2 presents recommended schedules for using each of the FCs. As Table 2 shows, the daily burden of performance evaluation is not cumbersome. You only have to review FCs 3 and 4 on a daily basis. If you have employees reporting to you, you also should review FC 5 each day. If you're having a lot of problems in one area, you should probably review your behaviors in that area a little more often at first. For example, if your boss is more than a normal problem, you might find it rewarding to review FC 4 after each meeting for the first week or so of your behavior modification program. This more intense review will give you immediate feedback and will heighten your awareness of critical performance deficits. FCs that deal with more "global" philosophical issues, such as FCs 1 and 2, should not be reviewed more than once a week. Your attitudes and

---

Table 2. Feedback Charts and Recommended Review Schedules

Feedback chart number	Performance area	Recommended review schedule
1	Your view of yourself and the world	Weekly on Monday at start of work day
2	Your attitudes and behaviors about work, organizations, your job, and coworkers	Weekly on Monday at start of work day
3	General demeanor	Daily at end of work day
4	Boss management and executive relations	Daily at end of work day or more often if lots of boss/executive contact
5	Employee supervision	Daily at end of day if you have employees to supervise, otherwise once a week at your convenience

philosophical orientations don't change much over the short term (barring momentous happenings), and it's pointless to check your progress in these areas more often.

It's a good idea to conduct your weekly reviews of FCs 1 and 2 at the start of the week's first work day. You're more likely to be optimistic and rested at the start of the week. It's a good time to monitor any dangerous tendencies to view the work world through the rose-colored glasses that high spirits sometimes wear. The best time to review your performances of day-to-day behaviors (FCs 3, 4, and 5) is at the end of the day and as needed if reviewed more often. This type of schedule allows you to look back over the day's events while your recollections are accurate. If you wait until the next morning to review the previous day's events, you'll find that your memories aren't as clear. In addition, the delay will distort your perceptions of the importance of individual events and your intuitive feelings about them. This type of data is invaluable in helping you to sort out and recall details.

Table 3. Sample Section of Feedback Chart 4

Target performance	Day				
	3/10 5:00 P.M.	3/11 9:00 A.M.	3/11 11:30 A.M.	3/11 4:20 P.M.	3/12 5:00 P.M.
12. Did you attempt to defend yourself when the boss was reprimanding you? (No = *)	NA	*	X	X	NA
13. Did you say anything negative to the boss? (No = *)	*	*	X	*	NA
14. Did you get your boss's work done first? (Yes = *)	*	X	X	*	*
15. Did you have feelings of friendship or human warmth toward your boss? (No = *)	X	X	*	*	X

The performance review process itself is very straightforward. Simply photocopy the FCs and label the columns under day or week to correspond to the appropriate review schedule (Monday through Friday for a daily review schedule or April 1 through April 29 for a weekly review schedule). In the case of "as needed" schedules such as using FC 4 ("Boss Management"), after each interaction with the boss fill in the *Day* section with the date and time as soon as you get back to your office and conduct your review. A sample section of FC 4 is shown in Table 3 as it might be filled out by Ms. Jones as she tries to shape up her boss-management behaviors. The boss is Ms. Jacobs. The displayed portion of FC 4 shows several days' worth of Ms. Jones's performance reviews as she monitored her boss-management activities. Ms. Jones had been having some problems dealing with Ms. Jacobs and had decided to implement her use of FC 4 after each interaction with Ms. Jacobs or at the end of the day if there was only routine contact by phone. The object on all FCs is to accumulate as many asterisks as possible. The asterisks represent good behaviors and attitudes in terms of the rules.

In Ms. Jones's case, things could be better. On March 10, she didn't have any meetings with Ms. Jacobs in person, so she filled out all of the FC 4 items at the end of the work day. The time, 5:00 P.M., is noted because following entries on the sheet might not be made at the end of the day. For FCs that are always filled out at the end of the day (such as FC 3, "General Demeanor"), the time would be superfluous. Under the March 10 entry, NA for "not applicable" was entered. Since Ms. Jacobs didn't do any reprimanding that day, it would have been pointless for Ms. Jones to claim an asterisk for not defending herself. During the several brief phone conversations she had with Ms. Jacobs on that day, Ms. Jones didn't say anything negative about anything, so she marked an asterisk next to item 13. Also on that day, she did all of her work for Ms. Jacobs before any other duties, so she earned the asterisk she gave herself next to item 14. Next to item 15 she had to give herself an X, the opposite of an asterisk, because she had briefly had empathetic feelings for Ms. Jacobs during one phone conversation. (Ms. Jacobs had mentioned that she had to be out of town on her anniversary, and Ms. Jones had fleetingly felt sorry for her.)

The next three columns all represent entries for March 11, when Ms. Jones had three in-person sessions with Ms. Jacobs. There had been a big screw-up in the Publications department, and Ms. Jones was taking a lot of flak. In her performance review right after the 9:00 A.M. meeting, she gave herself two asterisks and two Xs. She had avoided defending herself while being reprimanded and hadn't said anything negative (the two asterisks), but she got Xs for neglecting to get Ms. Jacobs's report done before completing her monthly report to Finance (one X), and she briefly felt sorry for Ms. Jacobs when J.B. yelled at her so loudly over the phone that Ms. Jones could hear it from the other side of the desk. At the 11:30 A.M. meeting, things were even worse. Ms. Jones broke under the pressure and tried to argue with Ms. Jacobs (the X for item 12), said something negative about the organization ("I can't be expected to fix things if nobody else around here cares about the product!"—an X for item 13), and, again, didn't get Ms. Jacobs's work done first (it wasn't something that Ms. Jacobs knew or cared about in regard to the problem at hand, but every detail counts—an X for item 14). It's not surprising that Ms. Jones got an asterisk for not having any feelings of human warmth for Ms. Jacobs after that series of meetings. After reviewing her earlier performance, Ms. Jones realized that she was making some dangerous errors. She pulled herself together and handled the 4:20 P.M. meeting much better. Except for a minor self-defense comment that earned her an X ("Well, I didn't know the people in Production Engineering expected me to do the checking"), Ms. Jones did well. Ms. Jones had no contact with either Ms. Jacobs or any other executives on March 12 (a good day), so she conducted only one FC 4 review at 5:00 P.M. There were two NAs because of the lack of contact with bosses or executives, one asterisk for getting Ms. Jacobs's work done before any other duties, and one X for some thoughts along the lines of, "Well, I guess Ms. Jacobs was only doing her job. I guess she's not so bad." A new FC 4 sheet would be started for the next day.

All of the FCs are scored in a similar fashion. A couple of points are important. First, you've got to use them regularly according to your set schedule. If you let the schedule slide or if you skip a day or a session here and there, you'll quickly end up abandoning the system. If you've got the feeling that this is going to happen, save yourself the trouble and don't bother in the first place. Second, you must be absolutely, completely, and consistently honest with yourself. If you cheat and take credit for unearned asterisks or avoid earned Xs, you're defeating the whole purpose of the exercise. If you can't even be honest with yourself when filling out the FCs in private, you won't be able to face up to the more fundamental issues: who are you, what do you want out of life, and what are you willing to do to get it? Third, don't tell anyone what you are doing. If others know about it, they may feel manipulated.

Don't get involved in a lot of recordkeeping. It's tempting to want to see how you're doing over time, but it's a waste of time to try. It's very complex to set up a system that allows you to track performances statistically like those on the FCs over time. In order to do it right, you have to have ratios of correct and incorrect behaviors to total behaviors, baseline periods in which you only measure and don't try to change anything, and so on. It's not worth it. All you've got to do is look over your performances for the last few reviews on a regularly scheduled basis and pay attention to the X items. You'll automatically feel good about the asterisk items, so don't even worry about them; simply seeing them will help you to increase them. If you find that you're having a lot of trouble in one particular area, take a few minutes to analyze the situation from every perspective. Think about what causes the problem, what is happening as it unfolds, and your behaviors and reactions at each stage. Think about your parental scripts and their possible influence. But don't get too involved in self-analysis. If you've got a nagging problem area, simply obey the appropriate rules without question, and you'll find that the problem will become easier to manage.

You have the power to modify your behavior in any way you want. Only you can change your destiny. You've now got the tools to do something about your business career. The only thing that can stop you is lack of hard work or a random stab in the back. It will be your own fault if you don't put up a desperate struggle to get what you want. If you decide to put that knife between your teeth and surge into the underbrush to hunt for success, good luck. Wave to us from the top when you make it.

Feedback Chart 1		(Page 1 of 2)		
Your Views of Yourself and the World				
Target	*Week*			
Performance				
1. Were you upset that "things aren't fair"? (No = *)				
2. Did you think you could be a hero? (No = *)				
3. Did you think your viewpoint was the same as everyone else's? (No = *)				
4. Did you think you were entitled to a break? (No = *)				
5. Did you think you had control over all the factors in the situation? (No = *)				
6. Did you fall prey to your own delusions? (No = *)				
7. Did you allow a script from childhood to direct your behaviors in a way you didn't like? (No = *)				
8. Did you take a chance and gamble on a long shot for something that wasn't a life-or-death issue? (No = *)				
9. Did you make little exceptions to the rules because the situation didn't seem important? (No = *)				
10. Did you think you were the only one with feelings of doubt and insecurity? (No = *)				

Feedback Chart 1 (Page 2 of 2) Your Views of Yourself and the World					
Target *Performance*	*Week*				
11. Did you have an honest discussion with yourself about your capabilities, performance, and chances? (Yes = *)					
12. Did you think someone else was watching out for you? (No = *)					
13. Did you overreact to a minor setback or triumph? (No = *)					
14. Did you get fooled by a first impression because you reacted emotionally? (No = *)					
15. Were you disappointed that you didn't get more recognition for the good work? (No = *)					
16. Did you think you weren't nice because you were following the rules? (No = *)					
17. Did you take something personally? (No = *)					
18. Did you expect some fun, satisfaction, affection, and achievement at work? (No = *)					
19. Did you fantasize about the incredible things you could do if they'd only give you a chance? (No = *)					

Feedback Chart 2 (Page 1 of 2) Your Attitude, Orientation, and Behavior toward the Organization, the Job, Coworkers, and Work in General					
Target Performance	Week				
1. Did you think everybody was enjoying themselves? (No = *)					
2. Did you play the game every second? (Yes = *)					
3. Did you believe the organization was carefully designed according to some overall plan? (No = *)					
4. Did you behave as if profits were the most important factor in decisions? (No = *)					
5. Did you stick up for your personal standards of honor and integrity? (No = *)					
6. Did you display intelligence and creativity just to show off? (No = *)					
7. Did you display aggressive behavior? (No = *)					
8. Did you only talk about how you value aggressiveness? (Yes = *)					
9. Did you try to change something just to make it work better? (No = *)					
10. Did you display disloyalty to the organization by word or attitude? (No = *)					

Feedback Chart 2 (Page 2 of 2) Your Attitude, Orientation, and Behavior toward the Organization, the Job, Coworkers, and Work in General					
Target *Performance*	*Week*				
11. Did you think the organization had a conscience, personality, or morals? (No = *)					
12. Did you try to play the game without a complete understanding of the rules? (No = *)					
13. Did you perform a behavior that demonstrated that you think people are more important than the organization? (No = *)					
14. Did you do anything to attack a part of the bureaucracy? (No = *)					
15. Did you try to push a change for your own purposes? (No = *)					
16. Did you get carried away and start to think that the technical job duties are more important than following the rules? (No = *)					
17. Did you demonstrate to everyone that you think the organization is a leader in its field? (Yes = *)					
18. Did you say anything negative about the way the organization operates? (No = *)					

Feedback Chart 3 General Demeanor Behaviors						(Page 1 of 3)
Target Performance	Day					
1. Did you keep complete control of your emotions in every situation? (Yes = *)						
2. Did you display exceptional courtesy to everyone? (Yes = *)						
3. Did you make any sarcastic remarks? (No = *)						
4. Did you try to be amusing or funny? (No = *)						
5. Did you try to cheat a rival? (No = *)						
6. Did you make a sexual remark, innuendo, or advance, even in jest? (No = *)						
7. Did you complain to anyone about anything? (No = *)						
8. Did you thank everyone who worked with you for their outstanding assistance? (Yes = *)						
9. Did you always appear busy and hard at work? (Yes = *)						
10. Did you become more informal and relaxed with someone? (No = *)						
11. Did you emulate the habits of the executives? (Yes = *)						

Feedback Chart 3	(Page 2 of 3)				
General Demeanor Behaviors					
Target	*Day*				
Performance					
12. Did you take action while you were angry? (No = *)					
13. Did you appear harried, upset, or flustered at any time? (No = *)					
14. Did you try to give the appearance of being concerned and sympathetic? (Yes = *)					
15. Did you get to work a little early? (Yes = *)					
16. Did you stay a little later than quitting time? (Yes = *)					
17. Did you consider the worst consequences of everything you were planning before you took action? (Yes = *)					
18. Did you smile at all times? (Yes = *)					
19. Was your work area always well organized, clean, and Spartan? (Yes = *)					
20. Did you use any profanities? (No = *)					
21. Did you dress conservatively? (Yes = *)					
22. Did you greet people formally and by their names? (Yes = *)					

Feedback Chart 3 General Demeanor Behaviors					(Page 3 of 3)
Target	*Day*				
Performance					
23. Are you in good physical condition? (Yes = *)					
24. Did you admit interest or talent in domestic areas? (No = *)					
25. Did you actively avoid mal-contents and trouble-makers? (Yes = *)					
26. Did you express nothing but enthusiasm for every-thing the organization is doing? (Yes = *)					
27. Did you participate in any clique activities? (No = *)					
28. Did you discuss or disclose salary data? (No = *)					
29. Did you solicit technical advice from your cowork-ers? (Yes = *)					
30. Did you associate with the current stars and organiza-tion heroes? (Yes = *)					
31. Did you admit to anyone that you were bored, angry, tired, or afflicted with any normal human emotions? (No = *)					
32. Did you offer or react to any opinions about any-thing? (No = *)					

Feedback Chart 4						(Page 1 of 3)
Boss Management and Executive Relations Behaviors						
Target	*Day*					
Performance						
1. Did you avoid executives at every opportunity? (Yes = *)						
2. Did you think executives were especially gifted? (No = *)						
3. Did you let executives know that you thought they were gifted? (Yes = *)						
4. Did you, however briefly, think that the executives would like to hear about problems? (No = *)						
5. Did you think that the executives understood what's going on at your level? (No = *)						
6. Were you surprised when the words and actions of executives didn't match? (No = *)						
7. Did you think that executives trust anyone? (No = *)						
8. Did you stay away from your boss at every opportunity? (Yes = *)						
9. Did you let your boss know how impressed you are by his or her work load? (Yes = *)						
10. Did you thank your boss for help and guidance? (Yes = *)						
11. Did you argue with your boss? (No = *)						

Boss Management and Executive Relations Behaviors

Target Performance	Day				
12. Did you attempt to defend yourself when the boss was reprimanding you? (No = *)					
13. Did you say anything negative to the boss? (No = *)					
14. Did you get your boss's work done first? (Yes = *)					
15. Did you have feelings of friendship or human warmth toward your boss? (No = *)					
16. Did you present your boss with any clear yes or no decisions whose answers you weren't sure of? (No = *)					
17. Did you give your boss credit for helping you with your successes? (Yes = *)					
18. Did you limit your maneuvering for attention to what was necessary only for your careful rule following? (Yes = *)					
19. Did you praise your boss at every opportunity? (Yes = *)					
20. Did you use your boss's pet insecurities to promote your programs? (Yes = *)					
21. Did you discuss your personal life with your boss? (No = *)					

Feedback Chart 4	Day				
Boss Management and Executive Relations Behaviors					
Target *Performance*					

22. Were you tempted to be open, honest, or candid with your boss? (No = *)					
23. Did you praise the quality of work that your people produce to your boss? (Yes = *)					
24. Did you try to prolong meetings with your boss? (No = *)					
25. Did you discuss unsolicited details of your work with your boss or an executive? (No = *)					
26. Did you go over your boss's head? (No = *)					
27. Did you tell your boss about unfavorable news that you heard about him or her or the department? (No = *)					
28. Did you assume that you could understand your boss's motivations and knowledge? (No = *)					
29. Did you attempt to promote your interests at the expense of someone else who reports to your boss? (No = *)					
30. Did you demonstrate nothing but enthusiasm in front of the boss? (Yes = *)					
31. Did you attempt to speak for the boss? (No = *)					

Feedback Chart 5 Employee Supervision Behaviors				(Page 1 of 3)	
Target *Performance*	*Day*				
1. Did you ignore your supervisory duties for "more important" work? (No = *)					
2. Did you assume that your employees should be as dedicated as you are? (No = *)					
3. Did you think that all of your employees were equally skilled and intelligent? (No = *)					
4. Did you reinforce your employees' awareness that it is important for them to talk favorably about their work group and you? (Yes = *)					
5. Did you let them know that you are fighting for their benefit with the organization? (Yes = *)					
6. Did you socialize with them? (No = *)					
7. Did you tell an employee something confidential? (No = *)					
8. Did you demean an employee? (No = *)					
9. Were you highly visible to your employees? (No = *)					
10. Did you act arrogant or condescending to any employee? (No = *)					

Feedback Chart 5 (Page 2 of 3) **Employee Supervision Behaviors**					
Target *Performance*	*Day*				
11. Were you candid with an employee about any negative information? (No = *)					
12. Did you try to impress upon your employees that management considers your department vital and important? (Yes = *)					
13. Did you think you could fool your employees about what's really going on? (No = *)					
14. Did you think what you said was more important than the example you set? (No = *)					
15. Did you give your employees a chance to make real contributions? (Yes = *)					
16. Did you put off dealing with a performance problem? (No = *)					
17. Were you more lenient with one employee than another? (No = *)					
18. Did you deal immediately with behaviors that you didn't like? (Yes = *)					
19. Did you think you could turn around any performance problem if you tried hard enough? (No = *)					

Feedback Chart 5 Employee Supervision Behaviors					(Page 3 of 3)
Target _Performance_	_Day_				
20. Did you discuss an employee's performance within earshot of another employee? (No = *)					
21. Did you foster the impression that you are the ultimate hire-and-fire authority? (Yes = *)					
22. Were you too liberal with praise or rewards? (No = *)					
23. Are you in complete control of the reward systems in your department? (Yes = *)					
24. Did you tell an employee about a promotion or other reward before you had final approval? (No = *)					
25. Did you give clear, detailed instructions for all tasks? (Yes = *)					
26. Did you compliment some of your employees for good work? (Yes = *)					
27. Did you ask anyone to perform personal chores for you? (No = *)					
28. Did you complete all employee-related paperwork on time? (Yes = *)					
29. Did you allow any of your employees to develop relationships with executives? (No = *)					

A

Appendix A
Topics from Social Psychology

Most of us like to think of ourselves as independent ships sailing on the sea of life. While we occasionally admit to ourselves that we have to put into port or interact with other ships, we like to think that we pretty much call our own shots. Those of you who have read Chapter 2 should realize that probability plays a large part in determining which opportunities we get a shot at and what results we get. I'm afraid that we have even less control than that. Almost everything we do in social situations (interactions with other people) is heavily influenced by principles of *social psychology* that are almost universal in their operation. The rest of this appendix and the following appendices on group dynamics and characteristics of organizations will demonstrate just how pervasive and persuasive these principles can be in influencing and controlling our behaviors. If you don't think so, put yourself in some of the situations described in this appendix, and see if you don't already act in more or less the same way. You'll see that many of the rules are intended to take advantage, in one way or another, of the situations created by people who blindly allow themselves to be directed by these social phenomena.

Social psychology is a large, complex, and rather diffuse field. It encompasses a wide range of overlapping and related phenomena that seek to explain the causes and results of interactions between people. One topic area of social psychology is group dynamics. Group dynamics is such an important topic that it is presented in a separate appendix. There are many additional areas of social psychology, each of which has its own extensive literature. While each of these additional areas has something of interest in terms of understanding the rules, they do not have enough practical applicability to warrant separate and detailed treatments in appendices of their own. This appendix will present some of the more interesting principles and findings from these other areas. Insofar as this is not a textbook on social psychology, I will omit the usual name and date references to the literature. Those of you who are interested can consult any basic social psychology text if you wish to read further. If you are a businessperson, you will get nothing of additional value from a detailed reading of the literature. I'll also omit as much of the jargon as possible.

The Primacy Effect

The most basic thing we do as animals is evaluate information about the world. We do not process this information with the objective, mathematical precision of a computer. Many of our most basic perceptions of the world are influenced by a number of social phenomena. One such influence is called the *primacy effect*. The primacy effect influences our assessment of an event's importance. It is evidenced by our tendency to attach as much (or more) importance to the order in which we receive information as we do to the actual content of the information itself. For example, consider the following descriptions of two people.

Person A: Intelligent, sensitive, hard-working, envious, crafty.

Person B: Envious, crafty, sensitive, hard-working, intelligent.

Now, quick—which one seems nicer, better? If you're honest, you'll admit that person A seemed nicer. Since you knew I was setting you up, you might have been a little suspicious and looked at the descriptions for a while before answering. Such a failure to follow orders will not help you in business. Of course, both lists of adjectives are the same, but if you gave a quick response, you probably thought person A sounded nicer. If you did, you would be in the majority. The reason for this differential attribution of niceness is that the initial few adjectives describing person A are "nice," while the first few for person B are not so "nice." Human beings have a marked tendency to attach extra significance or weight to information that arrives first.

The primacy effect has much significance in the day-to-day business world. Take first impressions as an example. Many of the rules are specifically concerned with generating the optimum first impression in the people around you at work. It's better to make no impression at all than to make a bad one. The first information people have about you will influence or act as a filter for all the later information they receive from or about you. If everybody gets a first impression of you as arrogant and impolite, every little sneer or grimace from you will only serve to confirm their initial perceptions. If, on the other hand, you were to make an initial impression as a polite, warm, and caring person, you'd probably have to punch out an elderly lady to change their minds. Remember, in the real world, everybody isn't going to be presented with a complete, accurate list of your characteristics. Your initial behaviors will be all they know of you. They will fill in the empty spots with what they've got.

Attribution Theory

Attribution theory is another interesting area of social psychology that is relevant to an aspiring rule follower. Attribution theories strive to explain how we perceive the causes of behavior, both our own and that of others. The central concern of attribution theory is whether a particular behavior is caused by internal factors such as personality type and mood or by external factors such as the expectations or presence of other people. In general, behavior that is unexpected or out of character for a particular person or situation is generally interpreted by observers as being caused by internal factors. Such unexpected information is assumed to contain more data about what the person is really like. For example, if the president of the company sends a check and flowers to the sick spouse of one of his managers, it's no big news; everybody would most likely assume the executive was just doing what executives are supposed to do. There would probably be little said about his personality just because he sends flowers. On the other hand, if the same executive was reported to spend every weekend nursing poor invalids on Skid Row, almost everyone would assume that it was the result of internal factors; the executive would most likely be perceived as "one hell of a nice guy," "salt of the earth," and so on.

The situation is reversed when we are attributing our own behavior. If we do something that we know is bad, such as padding an expense account, we tend to attribute the cause of our behavior to external factors ("Everybody does it," "The company always screws me, so they owe me," "They know but don't care"). When we do something good, such as donating money to charity, we generally attribute the cause to internal factors ("I'm a prince," "What a guy"). Many of the rules are specifically concerned with making sure that you help others generate favorable attributions about your behavior. If you do something expected, you want the observers at work to assume a favorable external attribution (you're acting like a responsible businessperson). If you do something unexpected (such as acting like a polished professional at all times), you want them to make a favorable internal attribution (you're a superior and insightful business intellect).

Don't underestimate the power of attribution effects. They work with and on each of us. One researcher conducted a study that demonstrated just how powerful these influences can be. The scientist and his colleagues admitted themselves to a mental hospital as patients. The hospital staff did not know they were psychologists. Having been labeled as schizophrenics in their records, they soon found that all of their previously "healthy" behaviors were attributed to their "mental illness." If they wrote a letter, it was recorded in their chart as "writing behavior" and thus representative of their disease. You can see how powerful the combination of the primacy effect and internal attribution was in establishing expectations in other people. The implications for work behavior are clear. For example, if a female employee were to be perceived as too aggressive, she could quickly be labeled as "pushy." All of her normal, assertive behavior in the future would then run the risk of receiving an unfavorable, internal attribution.

Attraction and Interaction

A number of topics are important in the area of interpersonal *attraction and interaction*. It's been pretty well established that if someone discloses personal information about himself or herself, other persons who are present will do the same. This natural tendency must be controlled. You don't have to answer every question put to you even though almost everybody else does. Think about what you want to disclose before you do. Remember, almost no personal disclosures at work are safe.

In most first-impression situations, *physical attractiveness* is the major determinant of whether the interaction will be viewed as favorable and worthy of further effort. In situations where there is additional information available about the person, the value of physical attractiveness declines. It's a good thing it works that way. Otherwise, only the beautiful people would get called back for second interviews. On the other hand, don't forget that almost everyone who interacts with you at work hardly knows you or your work at all. Most of them just see you walking by or talk to you once in a while. In these cases, physical attractiveness is a continually important factor. Do everything you can to enhance your personal appearance and to appear as the proper, professional business-person they expect and want.

Similarity is an important social factor. The bottom line is that people like other people who share their attitudes and beliefs. The more alike people perceive themselves to be in attitude, appearance, and personality, the more they will like each other. The implication here is that it is important for those in authority to perceive that you are just like them on as many dimensions as you can handle.

An interesting bit of research has implications for boss management. An experiment was performed in which subjects were asked to rate how much they like each of four different persons with whom they interacted privately for a short time. Each of the four people was in the league with the experimenter (these clandestine assistants are known as collaborators) and was following a strict set of instructions. One of the collaborators always said bad things about the subject to the subject, one said only good things, one started out saying good things and then got negative, and the fourth collaborator started out saying bad things but then switched to good things. The collaborator who was most liked by the subjects (on the basis of postexperiment testing) was the one who started out saying bad things but then switched to saying good things. This was true even though the largest number of good things was said by the "always good" collaborator. This explains why it is sometimes smart to pretend to argue with the boss for a moment before you revert to shameless groveling. Comments such as "You know, J.B., I wasn't too sure about your idea for the Jenkins deal at first, but now that I've had a chance to see the big picture, I'm really impressed" are excellent ways to demonstrate this "coming around" behavior in a short time.

We tend to like people who are physically close to us more than people who are farther away. This phenomenon is called *propinquity* by social psychologists. A large part of this attraction is the result of perceived similarity in interests, beliefs, and behaviors. For example, even if we don't know our neighbors very well, we tend to like them more than people in general who live five or six blocks away. If we see a neighbor walking through the neighborhood at 2:00 A.M., most of us would assume that he or she couldn't sleep or was out walking the dog. If we saw a complete stranger in the same circumstances, we'd probably check to make sure the door was locked. The fanatical devotion of sports enthusiasts to their home teams is in large part based upon our tendency to identify closely with nearby people and institutions. Such social tendencies undoubtedly evolved because it had survival value for our ancestors; the subhumanoids who didn't stick with and help the group probably ended up as food for some saber-toothed tiger. While there are few saber-toothed tigers in most organizations, the dangers faced by your career are no less savage. Understand your tendency to drop your guard and get close to people just because they're nearby. Remember, it's not us versus them; it's you versus the business world.

It's always interesting to listen to people talk about *conformity*. Conformity is a lot like stupidity; everyone agrees there's a lot of it around, but nobody believes they've got it. This view is encouraged by our myths and legends in which the hero is always a nonconformist who does things that few others would dare. Well, as with the legends concerning aggression, risk taking, and rule breaking, the legends concerning conformity are incorrect and dangerous if they are interpreted as providing rules for day-to-day business life. The fact is that an awful lot of conformity is absolutely necessary if you want to be a success. The rules show you the best ways to demonstrate this conformity. The danger with conformity is that you can't afford to conform blindly with the rest of the success-bound sheep. You must conform to group behaviors with a clear sense of direction and a full realization of what's going on. Most people just blindly go along with whatever is happening because they're insecure and can't handle the pressure of being different. That's just as dangerous as being recklessly nonconforming in order to show how tough you are.

The strength of peoples' fear of nonconforming was shown by an often repeated experiment in which groups of people sat in a room and estimated which of three lines was longest. Unknown to the one subject in the room, all of the rest of the people in the room were collaborators of the researcher. Whenever a set of lines was displayed to the group, the collaborators would give obviously incorrect answers, even though it was perfectly clear which line was longest. In study after study, from 20 to 40 percent of the subjects went along with the incorrect answer so that they would not appear different from the group. The implications for work are twofold and critical. First, everyone expects a lot of conformity because that's the way people usually behave. Second, don't allow yourself to conform without first evaluating the real payoffs and liabilities. In most cases, you'll find that you have to go along in order to make the right impression. In some cases, your initial objective analysis may save you from making a critical error, particularly in regard to situations in which the majority is recklessly breaking rules. A lot of people will break rules under the false assumption that they will gain acceptance from their peers or bosses. They may, but the trade-off in career damage more than offsets any short-term gains.

Compliance and Obedience

Aside from your primary goal of getting everyone to perceive you in the most favorable way, a lot of your business-related efforts are going to be directed toward getting people to do what you want them to do. Some research findings in the areas of *compliance and obedience* are directly applicable to the work environment. Research in general suggests that someone is more likely to do something for you if he or she owes you one, feels sorry for you, feels guilty about something he or she has done to you, and/or is frightened. It seems to help best if he or she is moderately scared. If a person is too frightened, he or she will freeze up and attempt to escape the situation rather than obey. If the person isn't frightened at all and other motivations aren't strong, he or she will just ignore you.

A very large part of getting people to comply with your wishes involves organizational roles and status (topics covered in more depth in Appendix B). Put in the most basic terms, people will obey and comply if they perceive that they are expected to do so. Their perceptions of these expectations are heavily influenced by the status of the order giver. A famous experiment illustrated just how powerful these expectations can be.

The basic situation involved a subject who was instructed to give a learner an electric shock if the learner failed to recall properly a list of words. The learner was in league with the experimenters and actually got no shocks. The subject was told that each shock given was greater than the preceding one. The upper ranges of the shock switch were clearly labeled "danger." Before the start of each session, the learner told the subject that he or she had a heart condition. The purpose of the research was to investigate just how far people would go in hurting someone before they would refuse to comply with orders. It turned out that quite a few would go all the way; about 60 percent gave the maximum shock.

In additional experiments, it was shown that many people would go all the way even though they could hear the learner pounding on the wall and screaming for the shocks to be stopped. A number of studies along this line yielded some interesting data. If the subject was paired with someone who refused to continue, the subject would most likely also refuse. If the subject was in the same room with the learner when the shocks were given, refusal was more likely. Overall, the findings demonstrated that people are more apt to obey when they are not faced with the immediate unpleasant consequences of their acts, when they are not supported by any social pressure to disobey, and when authority figures are close at hand. The implications for work are clear. Try not to put yourself in the position where your fate or programs are left in the hands of distant types who do not know you personally. Make sure that your people know that you are watching every move they make, however benign your presence. Make sure that you weed out the trouble-makers who provide social approval for behaviors that are counter to your success.

B

Appendix B
Group Dynamics

Society is comprised of large numbers of interrelated groups. While social psychology deals with all social phenomena, *group dynamics* deals specifically with the study of how behavior is influenced by the operation of group processes. Do not underestimate the influence that group processes have on your behavior. They're stronger than you think. Insofar as work activities involve many groups, a more detailed understanding of how groups operate will help you to apply the rules more successfully.

All groups have three basic characteristics: goals, roles, and norms. Groups form in order to perform certain functions or *goals*. The goals of a group may be explicit and clearly stated, or they may be rather nebulous and difficult for even the group members to define. In fact, many members of informal groups may not even know that they are in a group. This type of situation can be very dangerous at work if you aren't aware of what's going on. For example, the annual community charity drive committee in your town most likely has very clearly defined goals and objectives. Most of the members could probably state the goals in a straightforward manner. Contrast that with the group from the Marketing department that meets every day for lunch in the cafeteria. That group's members may not even realize that they are part of an established group, but they are. They would probably have difficulty arriving at a mutual agreement about what the group's goals are. To one it might be companionship at lunchtime, to another it might be a forum for complaining about the company, and to a third it might be a means of selling her ideas on what the organization should be doing. When there is no clear agreement among members about what the group's goals are, there are many opportunities for misunderstanding, disappointment, and frustration. Given the large number of informal groups of this sort that typically exist in an organization, it is no surprise that many of the rules are specifically designed to minimize the amount of time you spend in informal group activities.

Roles are the second important characteristic of groups. Roles are specific sets of behaviors that are performed by group members. Each group has a fairly rigid and consistent set of roles that are occupied by group members. For example, the president of a company typically has a role that requires that he or she be in charge, decisive, forceful, and experienced. In a family group, the father has a role that often requires that he teach the children "masculine" skills, mow the lawn, and take at least a passing interest in sports. Obviously, the role of father differs from family to family, but it is remarkably consistent over time within any one particular family. One person usually fulfills a number of roles at the same time. You could be a father, a husband, a manager, an engineer, a member of the softball league, and a Jaycee all at the same time. Each of these roles requires a different and often conflicting set of behaviors.

Roles can be broken down into three basic types. (Researchers have additional categories, but they are of research interest only.) The first type of role is the *enacted* role, which is the actual behavior the person performs, what's really happening. A second category of role is the *perceived* role, the role that the role player perceives or believes that he or she is filling. Finally, there is the *expected* role. This role defines the behavior that other group members expect to see from the role player. In the ideal situation, all of these roles will be the same for a specific individual in a given situation. For example, it could be that the president of a company is actually doing what the ideal president does (the enacted role), feels that he or she is doing the right things (perceived role), and is fulfilling the expectations of the employees, the board members, and the stockholders (the expected role).

In reality, of course, things don't work out that well. This is generally because each of the groups you work with expects a different set of behaviors, and your estimates of what each of them expects may be off a little. When the amount of discrepancy between role types is more than average, it's called *role conflict* or *role ambiguity*. If there is sufficient role ambiguity or conflict among group members, the group is affected adversely. Morale tends to be lower, productivity suffers, and individual satisfaction decreases. Role conflict explains much of what's euphemistically called "personality conflict" during termination interviews. The supervisor and the employee on the rack have conflicting views about the expected role the supervisor wants to see and the perceived role the employee is striving to display. The important point is to realize that just because you think you are fulfilling a role (perceived role) as the best middle manager in the organization doesn't mean everyone else sees it that way. In fact, you may actually be doing the job as it ideally should be done (enacted role), but key people may expect more groveling and less performance on the bottom line (a different expected role). It's not what you do but how well you perform the expected role behaviors that are in the minds of the key players. Do not make the mistake of underestimating the awesome power that role expectations play in shaping behavior and influencing peoples' evaluations of others' behavior. Just think for a moment of all the groups you interact with during the day and the various ways you behave with each of them. You not only say different things as you move from group to group but you also dress differently, use a different tone of voice, and display different body language. And you do these things more or less automatically once you've learned the norms of each group. Everyone else is doing the same thing and is also watching to see how you satisfy the behaviors they expect from you.

One of the most famous experiments in social psychology will demonstrate the power of roles to shape behavior. A group of male college students was selected to participate. The group was carefully tested to ensure that all of the finally selected subjects were within the normal spectrum of psychological and medical well-being. Coin flips were used to separate the subjects into two groups. One group was designated as the prisoners and the other as jailers. A mock prison was set up in the basement of a campus building, and the prisoners and the jailers were left to their own devices regarding how they would spend the week of the experiment. No other instructions were given. All they had to guide their behaviors was the presence of the prison and their own expectations of what prisoners and jailers were supposed to do.

The experiment had to be terminated early because of the surprising events that occurred. Almost immediately, the jailers began to brutalize the prisoners. They repeatedly rousted them out of their cells, made them walk blindfolded in a group to the bathroom, and herded them out of their cells for frequent inspections. The abuses were greatest when the researchers were not present late at night, and the jailers could let their role playing have complete expression. The prisoners, average college students who became prisoners only on the basis of a coin flip, did not rebel or argue with the jailers. Instead, they became docile, depressed, and compliant. Several of them broke down and cried when they were visited by friends and family members. Things got so bad that the experiment had to be stopped. None of the researchers had expected the role playing to become so extreme. In fact, the researchers themselves did not provide the impetus to stop the experiment, for they themselves had fallen into the role expectation trap (it's only an experiment, so what's the problem?). As the head of the study explained it later, a visiting graduate student was appalled by what was going on and was visibly shaken. Her reaction shook him back to reality, and he terminated the study. Role playing and expectations are even more powerful at work. People do it for a living, their egos are involved, and they've had years of practice. They know what they want, and you'd better give it to them or you'll be in big trouble.

The third important characteristic of groups is *norms*. Norms are the standardized rules of conduct for the group in general. They overlap to an extent with the behaviors expected from the specific roles people play. For some groups, norms are detailed and documented (as for the crew of a ship). For other groups, the norms are understood (as in most work groups). Norms serve several purposes. First of all, they provide group members with acceptable bounds for behavior; an individual doesn't have to deliberate endlessly about whether a certain behavior is OK; the group norms generally make it clear. People obey group norms in order to get social approval (spoken or unspoken pats on the back from other group members). The more valued the group is in the eyes of the person, the more that person will conform to the norms in order to get accepted. This is why it's very important to let work group members assist in developing procedures and policies; if they help, they'll value them more and will obey them more often.

Compliance with group norms depends on a number of factors. The lower the self-confidence or self-esteem of a person, the more readily that person will comply with group norms. Persons who continually deviate from group norms will soon find themselves shut off from the group. If you violate group norms, you will at first get a lot of attention from the group members (some of it unpleasant) as they attempt to bring you back into the fold. If you persist in your violations, you will end up out of the group. Major deviations from group norms are permitted only for individuals who have high value to the group and/or those who have shown a history of compliance with group norms. This is why an executive who screams and yells is tolerated. If such individuals have put in a lot of productive years and are valued, the group may permit them to be quite a bit different as long as they do not violate other important group norms. They have built up a surplus of what are called idiosyncrasy credits. If you are new to a group, you probably have relatively low perceived value and few or no idiosyncrasy credits. As a result, you have no maneuvering room; you'll have to scrupulously obey all group norms without exception unless your expected role permits some deviations (such as when you're a psychologist in a corporate environment; they often expect you to act a little strange so they'll think they're getting their money's worth).

Group size is a critical and often ignored factor that can enhance or limit a group's achievements. Research has demonstrated that, as groups get larger, several things happen. As a group grows to more than seven to ten members, subgroups emerge. This is a universal phenomenon across all cultures. It happens because groups larger than ten make it difficult for group members to communicate clearly and on the personal basis that members prefer. As these subgroups form, they begin to spend more of their time communicating within the subgroup than with the larger, original group. As a group gets larger, the group leaders begin to get more autocratic and less participative with group members. As the group grows, communications among members get more procedural and formal. These phenomena occur without exception and are most easily seen in work groups. Very illuminating examples can be seen among the Silicon Valley high-technology firms. Most of these organizations started as one- or two-person garage operations in which the principals were not titan-of-industry types. As the companies grew, many of them made vigorous attempts to remain informal and open. But it was a futile struggle. As the companies grew, it became more difficult for the founders to stretch their span of control wide enough to maintain one uniform set of norms. Subgroups sprang up and formed their own norms. Communications became more formalized as the founders began to communicate to the organization as a whole rather than personally with each worker. This further alienated the subgroups, which viewed such communications as less important than the subgroup's own activities. Little by little, these companies became more and more like every other company. They may still have beer parties on Fridays, and everyone may dress without regard for conservative taste, but on the more critical dimensions they are now us.

This is not to say that such processes are bad. After all, that's the way it works 99.99999 percent of the time. The problems arise when executives (and aspiring successes) try to pretend that such phenomena are not at work. Most executives prefer not to rise to the occasion as they wallow in the fantasy that their memos and pronouncements shape the style of the organization. In order to get the most out of an organization, executives must desperately struggle to reduce the discrepancies between the goals of each subgroup and those of the overall organization. At the same time, the subgroups must be nurtured and provided with the means to reward their members for outstanding performances. Subgroups will form, they can't be stopped, and they must be harnessed to get the most out of the organization as a whole. Countless studies have shown that smaller work groups result in increased productivity, higher morale, decreased supervision requirements, more opportunities for personal expression, and more creative solutions to work problems. The smart executive will use these groups to his or her best advantage.

Quite a bit has been written about *decision making*. Decision-making research attempts to understand how group processes influence consensus decisions by a group. It's an interesting area with direct relevance to the work environment. The most popularized aspect of group decision making seems to revolve around the perceived fact that groups always arrive at the safest, least risky decision. This isn't always the case. The term *risky shift* is used to describe group decision making that is more extreme and riskier (in terms of possible consequences) than decisions that individual group members would make on their own. The element that seems to lead some groups toward riskier decisions appears to be the group leader. In order to give the appearance of complying with group norms, members will often go along with what they perceive to be the leader's expectations. If the other group members are relatively weak and nonassertive, a risk-taking leader will heavily influence the group. If you are a risk taker, do not expect your employees to temper your decisions. They may go along just for the ride. If you are a member of a group in which such a process is operating, you may be stuck even if you know what's really going on. The leader may not want to hear the truth. Follow the appropriate rules carefully. It's not your problem if the organization makes a few (or a lot of) mistakes because some group went out of control. Your first concern must be your career. If you think you'll suffer badly as a result of some group's decision, be very careful about trying to influence the group's decision away from the popular choice. Most of the time, you're best advised just to go along for the ride.

Groupthink is the term used to describe the tendency of some groups to eliminate all dissent. At its most common level of operation, it functions to maintain group norms in the face of deviant behavior. At its most extreme, groupthink creates such strong pressure toward conformity that all critical and creative thinking in the group is eliminated. Those who attempt to fight this trend are quickly eliminated from the group. The characteristics of groupthink decisions are: (1) group members suppress any feelings of personal doubt about decisions that are made, (2) the group fosters the perception that it is morally superior to other groups, (3) the group feels it is impervious to outside effects, (4) the group believes that it will endure forever, (5) the group ignores information that it doesn't like or that is contrary to group policy, (6) there is very strong pressure to go along with the leader's decisions, and (7) the group maintains a high degree of enthusiasm for its actions and goals. History is rife with examples of groupthink in military and political situations. The business world's groupthink decisions are no less numerous although they may not make the history books. Please note that the rules do not advocate a yes-man posture. The rules do advocate a no arguing, no conflict, no ultimatum posture. If you are working for a boss who doesn't want to hear any dissent, you may not have any choice but to go along. Remember that it's really irrelevant whether your organization makes the best possible decision in the objective sense (such as what is best for profits or production). The best decision for you is the one that makes you look best. If that requires you to be a yes-person, do it and prosper.

Competition plays a major part in the actions and decisions of work groups. The manner in which group members perceive the outcomes of the competition can have a large influence on how well the groups perform. If one group is engaged in competition with another group (such as between two sales departments), individual group members will usually pull together and fight harder for their own group's success than they would if they were on their own. Morale and cooperation will increase, as will productivity. In order for this to occur, several conditions must be present. First of all, the group must have a well-developed sense of group cohesion. That is, group members must share common goals, know one another, perceive that each of them stands to benefit if the group succeeds, and have fairly frequent contact with one another. Failures to satisfy these conditions are generally the reason why sales contests between departments fail to produce results. Often, the departments or regions are comprised of salespersons who hardly ever meet, who operate independently, and who know that their own individual sales quotas are the only important thing to worry about. To such people, the term *department* or *region* as a sales group is a joke.

The other condition that must be present for the group to work together is that the group must perceive that the goal is not a zero-sum game. A *zero-sum game* is one in which there is a limited amount of rewards for performance. If one group member wins a lot, there is less for everyone else. In such a case, it makes little sense for the group members to work together; they know they're better off working for themselves. For example, if a group is told that the best producer will get the next promotion, do you think the management trainees are going to help one another? Don't count on it. In this case, the trainees are going to spend most of their time trying to look well and cheat one another. The fool who set up the zero-sum game will get less productivity than before in addition to destroying the helpful fabric of what used to be a cooperative group of management trainees. A smart contest designer would not mention promotion but would instead talk about across-the-board bonuses or salary increases if certain performance levels are attained.

C

Appendix C
Characteristics of Organizations

There is much confusion among psychologists, businesspeople, and the general public about the workings of organizations and the relationship between the characteristics of organizations in general and human social tendencies. Many people would have you believe that, because we are basically social creatures (we enjoy, need, and seek social contact), organizations and their operations are therefore natural extensions of the social behaviors we display in small groups (the family, bridge club, five children who hang out together). This assumption and the distorted evidence used to support it are dangerous and false.

Human social behaviors are the result of millions of years of evolution. Quite simply, our social behaviors exist because they had survival value for our subhuman ancestors. Small groups of these primitive creatures managed to survive much better if they helped one another and stayed close together. They didn't do it because they liked it; they were social because their genetic composition increased the tendencies for social contact. Perhaps creatures with the social gene required more tactile and auditory stimuli in order to feel comfortable. Whatever the cause of their inclination to practice social interactions, such contact meant that they had a better chance of surviving until they could produce offspring. Those of our ancestors who didn't have this tendency to form small, supportive groups lived alone and were killed off by predators before their genes could be passed to the next generation. If the genes that led to tendencies for antisocial behavior had survived instead of the ones we now have, perhaps humans would be solitary creatures like bears, who generally live alone and seek other members of their species only to mate. If that had been the case, you probably wouldn't be reading this book right now. It is hard to imagine how we would have been able to develop an advanced culture (language and written records) if we had been solitary creatures.

The problem with extrapolating from primitive social behaviors to human behaviors in current, large organizations like most businesses is primarily related to size. Organizations are so much bigger than groups that form naturally among people that they aren't just bigger; they're totally different entities. Normal social behaviors cannot be maintained homogeneously in human groups larger than about twenty people. Groups of primates in the wild are seldom very large either. It is rare to see a group, or tribe, of baboons or monkeys with more than 150 to 200 members. And these large groups have many subgroups (such as the young male group and the mothers with infants group) whose members spend the majority of their time with their own subgroup members.

Why is all of this so important? There's no reason to believe that the evolution and development of our social behaviors were any different from those we see in other primates today. Our primitive ancestors probably behaved in pretty much the same ways that we observe in baboon and monkey tribes. The only difference between us and them is our ability to think at a higher level. Our reasoning powers have led us to incredibly rapid technological advances that have created our present society. Cities did not form because we all like crowds, pollution, and crime. Our cities formed to support more effectively our developing agricultural and industrial activities. In a very frightening way, our abilities to think have created a civilization that is totally at odds with our innate social tendencies. We prefer small, close-knit groups, but most of us must live in huge cities where we don't know anyone. We prefer to limit our interactions to familiar people with whom we can form long-term relationships, but we're forever pulling up stakes and moving on to another job in another city where we know no one. We function best in stable situations where we can rely on past experience to provide us with easily determined, low-stress solutions to problems, but we are faced with a situation where knowledge is doubling every seven years and the personal computer you buy today will be a piece of outdated junk in two years. In short, we're totally out of our natural element. Evolution doesn't operate fast enough to reshape our social behaviors, so we are left to cope with the way things are today with social behaviors that were evolved to deal with an environment that ceased to exist in the last few thousand years. Indeed, evolution doesn't have much chance to operate on survival issues anymore, as we routinely permit and encourage even those with gross genetic handicaps to reproduce. In the absence of the brutal system of natural selection that weeded out genes that weren't optimum for survival, it's hard to imagine how our social behaviors will ever mutate genetically into a form more harmonious with the difficulties of modern life.

Yet, despite the incredible disparity between our natural tendencies and the environment we live in now, many people would have you believe that modern business organizations represent a simple and natural extension of the operation of primate social behaviors. Many books draw analogies between going to work and the hunting and food-gathering activities among early subhuman groups. The conclusion of these types of treatments is to argue that behaviors that fostered group cohesion and group success among primitive groups of primates will similarly foster your success and that of your business organization. But our current large business organizations did not evolve naturally; they are the result of practical necessity brought about by our technological skills. There was no need in the jungle for a group of 2000 subhumans to get together every day from 7:00 A.M. to 4:00 P.M. to work on a joint grub-digging project; such a mass gathering would serve only to trash the area and exhaust the grub supply. Yet we form such groups every day in order to process insurance claims, build cars, manufacture frozen dinners, and so on. Such large groups are the only economically feasible way we have developed to produce such items in the large quantities we must have. Just because we are required by our technological advances to do such things does not mean that our innate social behaviors led to the natural development of such large organizational systems. Further still, it does not mean that our innate social tendencies are designed to permit us to flourish or even survive in such a system.

Sometimes it is made to appear as if our natural social behaviors fit in quite nicely at work. This is merely the result of semantics. In any situation in which individuals behave, there will be a lot of group behavior and social interaction. It's easy to make the mistake of assuming that it's all natural and part of some larger overall plan. The simple, sad fact of the matter is that most of the social behavior that occurs in large organizations is the result of desperate attempts on the part of organization members to practice and maintain their "real," innate social behaviors— that is, the formation and support of small groups in which individuals can easily relate to and recognize one another. Large organizations do not provide such opportunities and, in fact, usually attempt to smother them.

While the behavior of organizations isn't a simple extension of small-group dynamics, it is remarkably predictable. And while natural social behaviors won't do anything good for you at work, it is important for you to understand how organizations tend to operate. This information is presented as an aid to your deeper knowledge and understanding so that you can more effectively follow the rules. Don't think that you can figure out a way to beat the organization at its own game. If you've read the rules already, you know your chances of changing an organization in a specific direction (other than random) or at a given pace (other than slow) are small. So don't waste your effort by trying. The purpose of this appendix is to provide you with a little more detail about how organizations typically operate. This information won't help you to do anything more effectively within the organization, but it may provide you with the ability to make more sensitive perceptions of the complexities and dangers you face in attempting to further your career in the middle of a ruthless organization.

Organizations are social systems composed of individuals and groups. The groups consist of both official groups (such as marketing, sales, and engineering departments) and unofficial groups (the coffee machine group, the complainers in Customer Service, the computer hacks in Finance). Organization leaders often fail to consider the tremendous influences that informal groups have on morale, performance, and general efficiency. In fact, as the earlier discussion in this appendix and the general tone of all the rules demonstrate, the goals of informal groups and individuals are often given more attention by organization members than the formal goals of the organization (such as making money or selling a deal). Organization members cannot relate to a large organization; it's not natural. In response to having to operate in such an impersonal environment, individuals form smaller groups as a natural, innate social instinct.

You don't have to look very far to see employees going to all sorts of extremes in order to advance the achievements of their informal work groups. Hence the incredible achievements of so-called skunk works, in which underfunded, somewhat clandestine efforts by close-knit groups turn out products that the parent organization couldn't hope to match. The skunks can do it where others fail because of the tight group bonds, the sense of getting away with something, the added challenge of having to appropriate money and equipment through unofficial channels, and the fun of it. It's ironic that the success of skunk works has led many companies to attempt to formally establish their own skunk works. Such efforts are doomed to failure. A skunk works with a formal organization chart, titles, policies, and procedures is just another department and won't produce any more than any other group of similarly intelligent employees working for the organization.

In the face of and usually totally oblivious of the spontaneous and immutable formation of informal groups, organizations have a number of mechanisms that enable them to pursue their formal stated goals. Organizations have sets of norms that outline in varying amounts of detail the behaviors that are acceptable for members of groups in various situations. Roles are prescribed sets of behaviors that individuals who occupy certain positions are expected to demonstrate. Each organization has a number of rigidly defined roles (such as president or janitor) that define the behaviors expected of people who occupy specific niches in the organization's hierarchy. Roles are discussed in detail in Appendix B. A further mechanism to motivate organization members is the organization's reward system, which defines the types and magnitudes of rewards that individuals occupying various roles can expect to earn if they obey the organization's norms and help it achieve its successes. The rewards range from the ubiquitous paycheck to perks such as offices, company cars, and expense accounts.

All organizations have the above characteristics in one form or another. The exact form of these characteristics determines the nature of the organization's style, its mode of operation, how it treats its people, what the physical environment looks like, and so on. Organizations are generally described as being somewhere on a continuum that runs from what can be called classical theory (CT) organizations (let's call these CTOs) and nonclassical theory (NT) organizations (let's call these NTOs). The theories don't explain many whys and don't even attempt any predictions, so they're not really theories. Since most organizational psychologists and their colleagues tend to discuss organization structure in terms of some type of CTO and NTO dichotomy, we may as well avail ourselves of the already established vocabulary. At the very least, you'll sound more learned the next time you have to trade jargon with some top-school MBA.

CTOs have the following types of characteristics: narrowly defined jobs, highly standardized and specific tasks within jobs, lots of policies and procedures, specialized training and background for persons hired for a job (they never take a chance on creative and unusual backgrounds in filling positions), restricted flow of information both to and from workers, a belief that workers can't be trusted, clear lines of authority with a worker having only one boss, pyramid-shaped organization charts with many levels of management, lots of workers at the bottom and few leaders at the top, and a narrow span of control (each boss only oversees a small group of workers). CTOs can be recognized by emphasis on routine, general disrespect for worker intelligence and potential contributions, authoritarian management style, and the tendency to organize along departmental lines rather than project lines. Most people work for an organization that has most of the above characteristics. Federal and state governments, large manufacturers, and most smokestack industries are typical CTOs. Some of the names associated with theories that explain or advocate CTOs are Weber's ''Bureaucracy,'' Taylor's ''Scientific Management,'' Fayol's ''Administrative Management,'' and Gilbreth's ''Scientific Management.''

At the other end of the spectrum are the NTOs. These are characterized by flexible and shifting lines of authority, a project rather than departmental structure, a much flatter organization chart than CTOs (less distance between the top and the bottom, fewer middle managers), a respect for potential worker contributions and input, diverse job duties and tasks that change over time, perhaps more than one boss per person depending on project demands, free exchange of information both up and down the lines of authority, a basic trust of employees, and decentralized decision-making authority. The most notable examples of NTOs are think-tank environments and, at least in their early stages, many of the high-tech firms in the electronics and computer industries. Some of the more well-known names in the world of NTOs are McGregor's ''Theory Y'' (as well as its CTO counterpart, ''Theory X''), Likert's ''1–4 Theory,'' Bennis's ''Organic Design,'' and Argyris's ''Personality and Organization Theory.''

Almost without exception, as organizations get larger in terms of members they slide toward the CTO end of the continuum. This occurs because the organization can no longer rely on natural group-dynamics factors to keep everything going in the same direction. Where the boss used to know everyone by name and everybody knew exactly where the company was going and what it stood for, all of a sudden there are 1,500 people walking around. Peoples' natural social instincts lead to the establishment of all sorts of small groups they can relate to with comfort and ease. The organization then has no choice but to start doing things on a more standardized and rote basis. Pretty soon, job descriptions get written by Personnel, and the once dynamic, tightly knit company becomes a bureaucracy. Of course, for a while, the bureaucracy will maintain some trappings of its more informal days, but soon even these fade. Before long, the founders are eased out and corporate types take over. It sounds sad, but it's not sad; it's just the way large organizations develop and mature.

It should be pretty obvious to even the most naive reader that it would be impractical for almost any large organization to attempt to be too NTO-oriented. Large organizations require quite a few standard systems and procedures just to let everyone know when the holidays are and to get the paychecks out. When it comes to attempts to communicate messages about how the company is supposed to present its image to customers, the situation is incredibly complex. In order to get large groups of people moving in something that can be called more or less the same direction, a lot of CT-type procedures must be applied. The problem is that there are all sorts of functions in every company that would best be served by an NT approach. The skunk works mentioned earlier are one such example. Believe me, the companies in which skunk works have flourished are among the most constipated, government-like bureaucracies you could imagine. But the narrow application of NT principles in such an environment was extremely successful. The same company might find that a skunk-works approach to payroll might not work out as well. Generally, task groups that are focused on research and development, rapidly changing markets or products, and analysis and experimentation are good candidates for NT approaches. Task groups that have to pump out a product are not good candidates.

The application of this knowledge for your own personal success requires you to understand and believe that organizations follow the above characteristics almost immutably. Organizations don't change very quickly unless they are threatened with immediate and total destruction (and sometimes not even then). If you haven't found the right spot in the organization you're in, don't make a mess of things by trying to push it where you want it to go. The only alternative to hanging in there is to pull up stakes and move on in the hopes of finding more congenial surroundings.

D

Appendix D
Reinforcement Theory in the
Real World

There are few middle managers and executives who have not attended seminars in which the elements of behavior modification and the concepts of reinforcement theory have been presented. In addition, a large number of consulting companies travel the country foisting half-baked behavior modification programs on organizational purchasers who feel they know enough to buy and administer such programs intelligently. As a result, everyone in the business world thinks that he or she understands the basic principles of behavior modification and knows how to apply them effectively in the workplace. They all talk about giving reinforcements and setting up contingency schedules like they know what they're doing. The sad fact is that very few people really understand anything about the basic principles of behavior modification in general, and almost nobody (including academians) knows what they're doing when they try to apply them in a work environment. This lack of knowledge on the part of ignorant practitioners is the main reason why most industrial behavior modification programs fail in the work world.

This appendix will be presented in two sections. The first will present the basic principles of behavior modification (sometimes called reinforcement theory, although it is a set of principles rather than a theory) as they were discovered in the laboratory environment. Most of the discussion will center on the principles as they apply to lab rats. This is appropriate in that 95 percent or more of all reinforcement research was initially (and probably still is) based upon the responses of lab rats. Once you have been exposed to the basic principles as they apply to laboratory animals, the second section will outline the challenges that

184

face a behavior modification program when someone drags the principles out of the laboratory and attempts to make them work on real, thinking people in a relatively uncontrolled environment.

In the Laboratory

The principles of *behavior modification* (B. Mod.) evolved over the last seventy years or so. B. Mod. and *reinforcement theory* are the same thing. Most of the research is done with lab animals. Although the primary subjects are usually specially bred lab rats, hundreds of other species have also been used as subjects. I will use the lab rat as the subject of discussion although the principles would be exactly the same for pigeons, dogs, monkeys, and so on.

The first principle of B. Mod. is to recognize that it can only be applied to what are called *operationally defined behaviors,* those that can be defined and described in purely physical terms. For example, to say that a rat "appears happy" is not an operational definition. To say that a rat "stood up on its back legs and licked its paws" is an operational definition of behavior. B. Mod. is not concerned with mental states, attitudes, or personal opinions. B. Mod.'s focus on operationally defined behaviors is both its strength and its great weakness. By using only operationally defined behaviors, B. Mod. applications can be very precise in defining and measuring behavior changes that large numbers of people can agree upon. The problem with operationally defined behaviors is that much of what motivates people's behavior cannot be operationally defined. People's expectations, their perceptions of social pressures, their attitudes, and their personalities all operate to influence behavior. B. Mod. only deals peripherally with these concerns.

The term and definition of *reinforcement* occupies a central position in the world of B. Mod. Reinforcement is only a definition. Many people do not understand this point; they erroneously think that reinforcements are a variety of objects such as money, food, or sex. While these things often serve as reinforcements (or reinforcers), they can be called reinforcements only if they meet the definitional requirements. A reinforcement is defined as an event whose occurrence increases the probability that the behavior it follows will occur again. For example, let's say that you are holding a rat that bites you on the hand, and you immediately give it a piece of food. The piece of food is a reinforcement only if there is an increased probability that the rat will bite your finger the next time you hold it. If, after a number of bites and a number of food reinforcements, you observe that the rat is savagely attacking your finger the minute you pick it up, you can safely assume that the food was a reinforcement. This distinction may seem artificial, but it only appears that way. In animal research, you'll generally find that what sounds like a good reinforcement usually is. It makes sense that food and sex would act as reinforcements to the typical hungry, horny rat. In most cases, they do. It's not always the same with people. The important thing to remember is that reinforcements increase the probability of the occurrence of the behaviors they follow.

The converse of reinforcement is *punishment*. Again, punishments are not things or events in and of themselves but are definitional. A punishment is an event whose occurrence decreases the probability of the occurrence of the behaviors it follows. Let's suppose that you're holding another rat for the first time. Since you're tired of getting bitten, this time you give the rat a noogie on its head after it bites you. If you find that after a few bites and noogies the rat stops biting your finger, it's safe to assume that the raps on the head served as punishments. Punishment is generally treated as if it were the exact opposite of reinforcement. In terms of definitions, it sounds that way, but in reality it isn't. There are some severe drawbacks to punishment as a means of inducing behavior change. Because punishments are generally unpleasant, they cause emotional reactions in the subject, whether the subject is a rat or an employee. An emotional response creates a situation in which the subject makes unfavorable associations about the experimental situation that will last long after the experiment is over and the behavior in question (here the biting) is eliminated or decreased. For example, if you have a very persistent rat who keeps biting your finger despite many noogies, that rat will end up receiving a lot of punishment (the noogies on the head) before the biting behavior decreases. Once the biting stops, you may find that you have another problem: The rat hates your guts. When you reach into the cage to get it, the rat will smell that it's you ("Oh, no! It's noogie person!") and will have an emotional response: It will defecate and urinate, cower in the corner, and maybe just freeze in one position. Your use of punishment will have created another whole set of behaviors that now have to be dealt with before you have a friendly, well-adjusted rat.

Before introducing the next topic, it's necessary to discuss lab equipment for a moment. The main piece of equipment used to conduct B. Mod.

research is called a Skinner box. It is named for the founding father of
B. Mod., B. F. Skinner. The Skinner box consists of an enclosed cage
that is usually designed so that the animal cannot be distracted by things
happening outside the box. The inside of the box usually has a bar that
the animal must press to obtain rewards and a tube or chute through
which the reinforcements are delivered. The bottom of the cage is usually
wire mesh through which electric shocks are sometimes given as punishments. Depending on the B. Mod. research, the box may be variously
equipped with buzzers, lights, trap doors, and so on. In the most
common type of B. Mod. research with rats, bar pressing is the variable
that is observed as a function of food pellet reinforcements delivered
through the food tube.

You may wonder why lab rats would be so interested in pressing a
bar to get some food. The issue is one of motivation. In almost all B.
Mod. research, the lab animals are given food as a reward. In order to
make sure that the animals are highly motivated to work for the food,
the animals are brought down to what is called criterion weight. This
is a euphemism for dieting them down to about 80 percent of what they
would weigh if they were allowed to eat as much as they wanted. The
result is an animal that is highly motivated to get something to eat. The
animals are maintained at criterion weight over the course of the research
by subtracting what they get during the experiment from the remainder
of their food allowance. This ensures that even a hard-working, much
reinforced rat cannot gain weight. Thus, the animals are highly motivated,
and they stay that way throughout the research. This may seem like a
minor point, but it is not, especially when real-life applications are
designed. Few B. Mod. programs in work environments can maintain
workers' motivations at a level that corresponds to the high motivation
levels of lab animals in food reinforcement studies. Academians and
consultants seldom mention this constraint. The next section of this
appendix deals with this problem and several others that are just as
critical.

The terms *positive* and *negative* are often used with the term *reinforcement* as in negative reinforcement and positive reinforcement. *Negative
reinforcement* is almost always used incorrectly. It's been misused by
magazines, by actors playing psychologists in movies, and by great
numbers of consultants, executives, and personnel types. It's not an
earth-shaking problem, but you have to wonder how much these people
know about applications if they can't even get the definitions right. The

terms *positive* and *negative* have nothing to do with whether the reinforcement or punishment is good or bad; the term *positive* merely means that a stimulus has been added to the situation, and the term *negative* merely means that a stimulus has been taken away from the situation. For example, in the situation where you gave the rat a piece of food each time it bit your finger, you were providing positive reinforcement. It was reinforcement because it eventually led to an increase in finger bites. It was positive because you added the food to the situation; it was not positive because the rat liked it or because it increased the finger bites.

The most frequent misuse is of the term *negative reinforcement*. Most people think that negative reinforcement is punishment, something bad that the animal will not like. Remember, the term *reinforcement* means by definition that the stimulus results in an increase in the behavior it follows. *Negative* means that a stimulus is being removed from the situation, and the removal of it leads to an increase in the behavior it follows. For example, let's say that another one of your rats has just been put into a Skinner box and you're trying to train it to move toward the bar. Your goal is to get it near the bar so you can train it to press the bar. Bar pressing is not something that rats will do on their own, so they have to be trained before you can even start a real experiment. In the background, a high-pitched buzzer is droning on and on. Rats don't like high-pitched, loud noises any more than we do. Every time the rat turns toward the end of the box where the bar is, you turn off the buzzer for three seconds. If you find that the number of turns toward the bar increases, then the removal of the noise is a negative reinforcement. It is negative not because the rat didn't like it, but because it was removed from the situation.

There are also positive and negative punishments. *Positive* and *negative* have the same definitional requirements in the case of punishments that they have with reinforcement. A positive punishment is one in which the addition of a stimulus to the situation leads to a decrease in the target behavior. The noogies on the rat's head (the addition of pain) acted as a positive punishment in the earlier example. A negative punishment is one that decreases behavior through the removal of a stimulus. A common example of a negative punishment is making a child who talks back stop watching TV and sit in a corner. The removal of the TV would be a negative punishment if the frequency of backtalk behavior decreased.

As I mentioned above, rats do not press bars instinctively. If you want to do an experiment involving bar pressing, you first have to teach the rat to press the bar. The process of doing this is called *shaping*, the reinforcement of successively closer approximations to the target behavior. In the above example, we were using negative reinforcement (the removal of a loud buzzer) to train the rat to turn toward the bar. Instead of negative reinforcement, let's use positive reinforcement with food, since we'll be using food as the reinforcement in other examples. When we first put our criterion-starved rat (80 percent of normal weight) in the box, it will sniff, explore, and generally trash up the box by urinating and defecating. I have never heard of a rat that just went over and pressed the bar. To begin the shaping, each time the rat turns its head toward the bar even a little, a food pellet is delivered through the food chute. Since this chute is usually near the bar, the delivery of the first pellet is a big help in getting the rat to hang around near the bar. For the next few trials, a food pellet is delivered for head turns toward the bar. After a number of reinforcements, the rat will be constantly looking over its shoulder toward the bar. Then you get more demanding and require the rat to turn not only its head but also its upper body. When the rat is doing this regularly, you then require it to be facing the bar before it gets a pellet. Little by little, you shape the rat to the point where it only gets a reward for touching the bar with its body, then touching the bar with its paw, and finally for pushing the bar. This shaping process can take anywhere from fifteen minutes for a lucky and smart rat to three or four hours for a slow learner. While shaping is obviously absolutely essential for B. Mod. programs involving rats, it is also very useful in shaping the behaviors of workers, children, and so on.

In all of the above examples, the animal received a reinforcement or punishment each and every time it performed the target behavior. This arrangement of consequences is called a one-to-one (1:1) contingency schedule, meaning that the subject receives one reinforcement or punishment every time the target behavior is performed. A 1:1 schedule is essential during shaping and early in the conditioning process. The 1:1 schedule allows the subject an opportunity to learn most effectively the relationship between the behavior and the consequence.

However, a 1:1 contingency schedule is not the most efficient schedule to use if you wish to build up a strong and long-lasting behavior through reinforcement. Once an animal has learned the basic target behavior, a much stronger and longer-lasting response pattern can be developed if the animal is given less than one reinforcement for every performance of the behavior. In the case of the rat in the Skinner box, this would mean that a food pellet might be delivered only after two or three bar presses. If one food pellet was given for every five bar presses, the rat would be operating under a 1:5 reinforcement schedule. It is possible to reduce gradually (the process is called thinning) the number of reinforcements to as much as one for every 200 responses, or a 1:200 reinforcement schedule.

The amazing thing is that the higher the schedule (the more presses required to earn a reinforcement), the stronger the learning becomes. The manner of determining the strength of learning will be discussed in a moment. There are a number of types of reinforcement schedules. If the rat is given one pellet after every fifth bar press, it is operating under a 1:5 fixed ratio schedule. If the food pellet is delivered after every fifth bar press on the average, the rat is being trained on a 1:5 variable ratio schedule. A fixed interval schedule would yield a pellet every one, two, three, or four minutes. There are many different types of basic reinforcement schedules (Skinner listed sixteen primary ones) and hundreds of combinations.

Reinforcement schedules are more than just academic curiosities. Think for a minute about how most of us receive reinforcements in everyday life. We're hardly ever on a 1:1 schedule. We get paid every week at best, but we're required to work all week for it (a one-week fixed interval schedule). We hardly ever get told that we're doing a good job by the boss even though we're supposed to work hard all day every day (for some bosses, this is about a 1:10,000 variable ratio schedule, but with no shaping or response-building period). The reason why particular reinforcement schedules are important is that learning is stronger with some schedules than with others. The strength of learning is measured by extinction. *Extinction* takes place when the subject is allowed to respond and no reinforcements are given. Once your rat was trained to a particular schedule, the strength of the bar-pressing response (and thus the efficacy of reinforcement schedules) could be measured by extinguishing the bar presses. The rat would be placed in the Skinner box, and no food pellets would be given. This process would be continued for a hour or so each day until no further responses were observed. It turns out that 1:1 schedules extinguish very quickly. This makes sense in that a few nonreinforced bar presses would provide the rat with a lot of information about the way things were working. In general, variable ratio and interval schedules lead to responses that are remarkably resistant to extinction. Very complex schedules that employ both decreasing and increasing variable ratio schedules have produced response tendencies in pigeons and rats that were so strong that more than 10,000 nonreinforced responses were performed before extinction occurred.

Two interesting phenomena point out some of the subtle complexities of learning. If you were to extinguish fully your rat's bar-pressing response and then put the rat back into the Skinner box two weeks later, you would most likely observe something called *spontaneous recovery*. The rat, which had been fully extinguished, would press the bar a few times. No one knows why this occurs; the theories are interesting but have no real-world relevance to B. Mod. applications in the workplace. The other interesting phenomenon involves retraining. If you were to put your rat back into its cage, just let it sit around for a few months, and then attempt to retrain it to press the bar again, you'd find that the rat would require much less training (fewer reinforcements) to relearn the bar press. This phenomenon occurs in humans as well and demonstrates that nothing is ever completely forgotten once it is learned.

Extinction through the use of punishment is much more complex than extinction through the withdrawal of positive reinforcements. As stated earlier, punishment is not the opposite of reinforcement in anything more than concept. The effects on rats are very complicated in terms of punishment's effect on the rate of extinction. It works to eliminate the behavior, but it causes emotional responses that create further problems. In the real world, with people, it's a different story, as you'll see in the next section. Punishment is but one area in which laboratory findings are at odds with the way it works in the real world. Let's look now at some of the other reasons why a lot of B. Mod. programs don't make it in the real world.

In the Real World

Alas, the laboratory is not the real world. And rats are, with few exceptions, not employees. If you could keep these two points in mind and recognize their implications, you'd probably explode in a fireball of insight into why B. Mod. is almost never used properly in business. B. Mod. concentrates entirely on operationally defined behaviors. To staunch proponents of B. Mod., if something isn't observable as a behavior, it isn't worthy of attention. With rats, pigeons, young children, and puppies, this orientation is fine. With adults and children over about the age of seven, it's a serious problem.

The behavior of human beings is stimulated, influenced, and modified by a lot of things that aren't readily observable. If you've already read Appendices A and B, you understand the incredible power of social pressures and internalized social norms in shaping behavior. The typical B. Mod. program in industry does little to affect these underlying social influences. In addition to the powerful influences of group dynamics, there are differences between people in terms of their early upbringing (their internalized scripts), moral values, religious beliefs, and motivation from moment to moment. Every one of our behaviors is filtered, processed, evaluated, and modified by many internal, unique values and points of view before it is displayed to the world as a behavior. The typical B. Mod. program ignores these very powerful and personal influences.

Let's talk about punishment for a moment. Most work-world B. Mod. programs attempt to use positive reinforcement as a behavior change agent. But on a day-to-day basis, positive punishment is used a lot more often than anything else in attempts to modify behaviors. This occurs even in organizations that have ongoing B. Mod. programs in force. Just look at the type of feedback most employees get from their supervisors. If the employee is doing well, he or she hardly ever hears anything. This constitutes a lack of positive reinforcement for desired behaviors. Fortunately for civilization, many employees provide themselves with a lot of internal reinforcements for doing a good job. But when something goes wrong, the roof falls in and the employee gets reprimanded, which is positive punishment. There are many reasons why such punishment is not effective. As mentioned earlier, punishment generates emotional responses. If you yell and scream at an employee enough or embarrass the employee or ruin his or her self-esteem, the employee will begin to make some unpleasant associations about you. The employee will begin to do one or more of several things, including avoiding interactions with you, saying bad things about you to others, working to the letter but not the intent of the regulations, and letting little things go by that will cause problems later but for which he or she won't be blamed. These responses are just what you don't need, especially with a problem employee. A more basic procedural problem with punishment is that you can't give it often enough to make it work. With people, you must administer a punishment every time the undesired behavior occurs if you want to establish conditioning. In a work environment, you can't possible provide enough supervision to catch all the undesired behaviors in order to administer consequent punishment. If you were to punish every fourth response (and catching that proportion of bad behaviors would be quite a feat of supervision), you'd end up increasing the strength of the response rather than decreasing it. This will occur because the person would be getting some sort of internal reinforcement (such as patting himself or herself on the back for doing the "right thing") the other 75 percent of the time. You'd have, in effect, a simultaneous reinforcement–punishment contingency schedule in which you're providing the punishments 25 percent of the time and the person is providing or getting some type of reinforcement the other 75 percent of the time. The punishment won't have a chance. In fact, the punishment (typically a verbal reprimand) usually only serves to get the employee angry and worsen the situation, especially if other employees are perceived to be getting away with something the punished employee got caught for. So you can't win with punishment even if you try.

Let's take a look at the reinforcement that people most often work for. Is it food? Probably not. After all, there are few (statistically speaking) people in the United States who are wondering where their next meal is coming from. Most people probably wouldn't work much harder if food chutes were installed next to their work stations so that they would get a food pellet if they did good work for fifteen minutes (although quite a few people would probably benefit by being brought down to criterion weight). Is sex the reinforcement? Probably not. Although the availability of attractive members of the opposite sex might stimulate some short-term increases in productivity, most of us would have trouble handling more than a few reinforcements a day. So-called *primary* reinforcements such as food, shelter, sex, or water are not very effective in increasing target behaviors because few employees perceive that they are in a state of deprivation in regard to them. In fact, even money (which is really a secondary reinforcer but acts like a primary one) isn't that effective. After all, as long as employees are employed, they get paid. The small extra amount that is typically used as reinforcement in B. Mod. programs doesn't mean that much to anyone. If employees were not paid anything except what they earned as specific reinforcement for target behaviors, it would be a different story.

What do we work for, then? We work for what are called *secondary* reinforcers. When we were children, we were oriented almost completely toward primary reinforcements. Food, warmth, cuddles, diaper changes, and such things were our only wants. Almost immediately, we began to associate the delivery of primary reinforcements with the presence of our parents. As we developed, we began to form primitive concepts of self and others that were heavily influenced by our early experiences in obtaining primary reinforcements. It is this pairing of the arrival of primary reinforcers with secondary reinforcers that creates civilized adults. In only a few months, a toddler will stop poking the dog in the eye just on a "Bad, Johnny, bad!" from Mommy. After a while, the child develops an internalized set of concepts that map out how secondary reinforcements can be earned. In this way, each of us develops a set of prides, fears, hopes, values, morals, and beliefs that are influential in shaping our behaviors in response to the outside world. Given the above, it is easy to see that people work for the satisfaction of a host of secondary reinforcement needs. Rule 81 presents data that demonstrate just how important these secondary reinforcements are to employees. Employees require secondary reinforcers such as a feeling of involvement, a sense of achievement, a belief that they are making an important contribution, and a belief that they are growing as professionals and caring individuals.

Even if you were to do everything correctly, you're still not out of the woods in terms of motivating your employees to work for secondary reinforcements. In case you haven't noticed, your employees' offices are not Skinner boxes, and you're not able to return your employees to the controlled environment of a rat colony after the work day. The consequence of this state of affairs is that you have relatively little control over the amounts of secondary reinforcements they can obtain from nonwork sources. They may be getting so much satisfaction from their private activities that they could care less about working extra hard for secondary social reinforcements at work. In fact, as we'll see, you don't have much control over the types of secondary reinforcements that are given at work right under your nose. Given these and other considerations, let's take a look at how most B. Mod. programs in industrial and commercial environments are set up and run.

Ninety percent of B. Mod. programs in business environments can be divided into two types: those that are almost passing afterthoughts that nobody pays much attention to and that die after a few weeks or months, and those that are set up with a great deal of hoopla, management training, and administrative work and that die after a few weeks or months. The first type deserve no attention at all; these are programs in which the top executive or purchasing manager is merely attempting to slick the troops with a PR, rah-rah move. Such tactics probably didn't work very well forty years ago, and they most certainly won't work now. Let's examine the typical B. Mod. program as it is set up with a lot of fanfare and administered in a business setting.

B. Mod. programs are typically purchased by high-ranking corporate or divisional officers to solve operational problems that have come to these individuals' attention. This in itself is a very serious liability. High-ranking officers of an organization seldom know what's really going on, and they almost always think that they can direct changes in the organization just on their say-so. As a result, when they decide to buy or allow themselves to be sold a B. Mod. program, they automatically think that they have identified the real problems, and they believe that if they announce the program and get it started, it will work.

Every B. Mod. program must have target behaviors to change or modify. Program purchasers are usually concerned with a variety of middle-management behaviors that they would like either to eliminate or to increase in frequency. Most of the time, the target behaviors that are selected have little relationship to the real problems the organization is facing. For example, a very popular brand of B. Mod. programs focuses on productivity. All sorts of operationally appearing indices of good management–employee behavior are listed and charted as part of the program. The problem is that most of these types of indices are once or twice removed from actual, day-to-day employee behavior; they're results rather than behaviors.

Consider one program that I had the misfortune to examine up close. The participation of this organization's Customer Service department was typical of the approach used in all departments. The behaviors that were tracked were the number of total phone calls handled by the department each week, the number of phone calls handled per hour per person, the number of sick days for the department per week (this had been a problem), and the number of dollars per adjustment given by each representative per week. At first glance, these all seem like reasonable items to track, but these indices are not behaviors. They are results of behaviors, and not very informative ones at that. Who cares if one representative is taking more calls per hour? The concern should be on the quality of the call, how it is handled to maximize customer satisfaction and, secondarily, to keep costs under control. You're not going to be in business long if your customer service reps are being unnecessarily tight with justifiably angry customers and driving them away in the process.

And if you've got a problem in the area of sick days, either you're hiring losers, you're not paying them enough, the working conditions are lousy, or the employees are not getting the proper guidance and training, all of which are your own fault.

If it were my Customer Service department, I'd track the behaviors that influence the desired results. Among them would be the following: whether and how often proper training and guidance are given to reps by the department supervisor, how often the reps are handling the calls with the proper courtesy and according to policy guidelines, how often the supervisor provides proper feedback to the reps, and how often the reps are asking for help when they need it. These are the behaviors whose frequencies I'd want to increase. Of course, I'd also be concerned with such items as cost per adjustment and calls per rep, but only after the above behaviors were monitored and I was happy with them. Among other things, I'd like to know whether the customers feel they are being dealt with fairly, whether the customers will do business with the firm again, and just what is causing the Customer Service problems in the first place.

Few programs go after these behaviors and results. You can probably see why. My list of behaviors and results would be an awful lot of trouble to observe and measure. The more often studied calls per hour and other nonbehaviors can be taken easily from computer outputs. Another difficulty with doing it the right way is that one begins to see that the behaviors under study are not isolated to the Customer Service department. After all, if you're going to observe whether reps handle calls according to policy guidelines, someone is going to have to develop comprehensive guidelines that consider cost–benefit trade-offs between customer satisfaction and adjustment dollars. Further, someone will have to make sure that the supervisors are properly trained. On a more basic but operationally complex level, someone is going to have to actually walk around and observe behaviors in action rather than take figures from a computer printout. Worst of all, what if you find that the customer reps are doing a great job but the problem is with the quality of your product? Now you've got an organizational problem and one that can't be summarily laid at the feet of the poor drones in Customer Service. You can see why most B. Mod. programs stick to the useless but easily measured nonbehaviors that are recommended by the consultants: It keeps everyone out of trouble. Well, there's no need to get into trouble. If you're not going to do it properly and get actual, honest results that will help you do your business better, why spend the money in the first place?

After the behaviors are selected, the next stage involves the specification of the reinforcements that will be distributed to employees when they perform the target behaviors. The other appendices and the earlier parts of this one make it crystal clear that secondary reinforcers are the rewards for which employees work. Given this undeniable fact, what rewards do most B. Mod. programs provide? You guessed it: relatively worthless reinforcers such as microwave ovens, trips to Hawaii, or golf clubs. And these are the "big-spending" programs. The cheaper ones give away movie tickets, baseball caps, or points that can be used to buy earrings, blenders, tires, and other items from a catalog. I've heard many white- and blue-collar workers indignantly complain, "They tell me to be a professional, and then they try to bribe me into working harder by giving me a shot at a blender?" They then go on to complain about all of the more basic problems their organization has and that they perceive the executives are too stupid to do anything about. The problems with these types of reinforcements are legion. Not only do they not appeal to needs for achievement, involvement, or a sense of accomplishment, but they wouldn't work even if everyone was motivated to work for them. They are usually available only to a small portion of the people who work for them (as when all good performers get their names put in for a drawing). This reduces the perceived relationship between the performance of the behavior and the reinforcement. When there's a big time lag between the performance of the behaviors and the arrival of the reward, there's a tendency on the part of the employee not to keep the behavioral requirements in mind as he or she works. Thus, the employee does a lot of work at times when the operational definition (how to do it) of the target behaviors and/or a desire to earn the reward are not kept in mind.

While the above problems are sufficient to completely compromise the effectiveness of most B. Mod. programs, they are not the biggest and most serious obstacles. The killer blow to most industrial and commercial B. Mod. programs is the failure of program designers to compensate adequately for the effects of the existing social structure and the reinforcements it provides to the employees. Every organization has a complex set of norms and roles that define the behaviors that are acceptable to the organization. These norms and roles determine who gets rewarded and for what behaviors. Almost always, B. Mod. programs are installed without considering or compensating for the effects of these existing reward structures. I've seen all sorts of programs where middle-management efficiency was the target. Dozens of results of behaviors would be charted, but the organizations were still poorly run and inefficient. Everybody knew the real score: You play along with the B. Mod. program and show you're on board, but you continue to operate as usual. For a B. Mod. program to have any real impact, it has to operate on the very social fabric of the organization. The target behaviors have to be the very basics: proper guidance to employees from the chairman on down, work done right and on time, cooperative behaviors with all employees, delegation of responsibility and authority, and so on. The problem is that few executives are willing to allow that much change, and, even if they were, they would contend that everyone but them (and their head-shed associates) needed it. As a result, the same old signals would be sent out of the organization, and the program would fail.

Given the foregoing, you're probably wondering if any B. Mod. programs ever work in the real world. Not many do. I'd say that fewer than 1 percent have any real impact after the first six months. Initial gains are usually the result of heightened awareness and novelty effects. You could spur some initial but short-term increases in productivity in any work situation simply by having someone walk around and yell "Work harder and manage better!" every half-hour. If you're not going to do it right, save yourself the trouble and expense and the very real damage that another failure will do to the morale of your employees. Forget B. Mod., and buy some new furniture for the executives. At least you'll get something for your money.